AF506265

'Gras'

'Gras'
Erik Steinbrecher
Photographs 1993–2002

Edition Patrick Frey

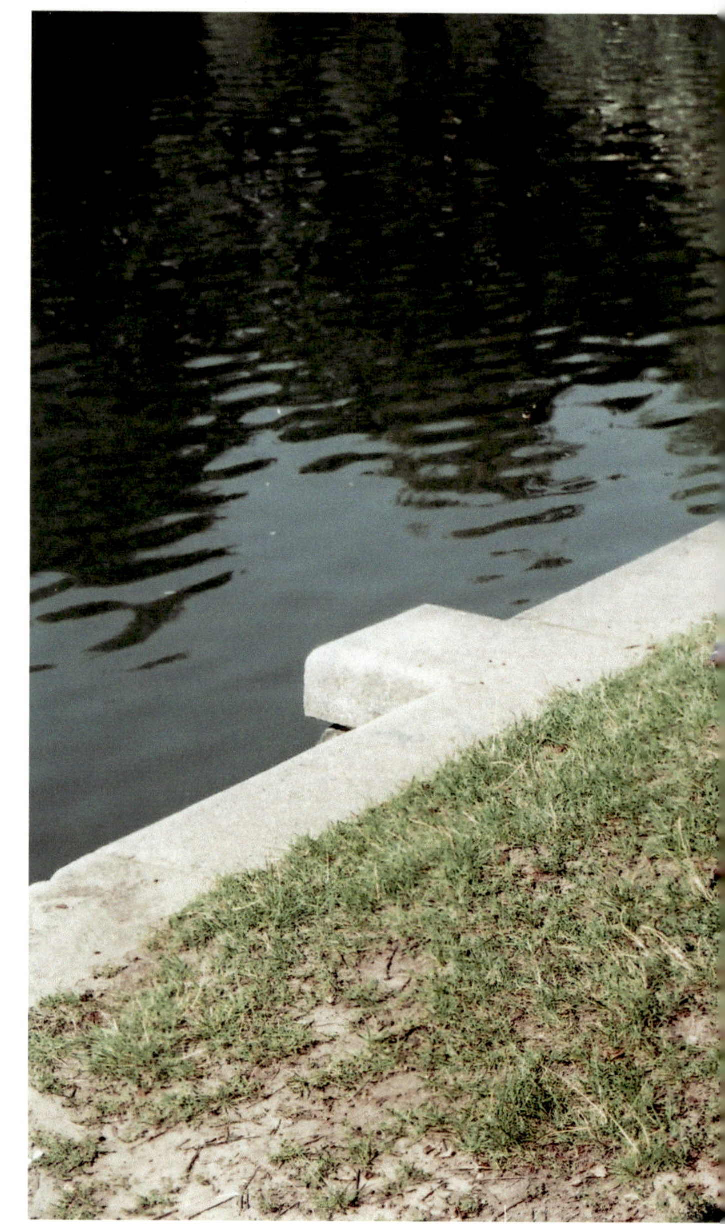

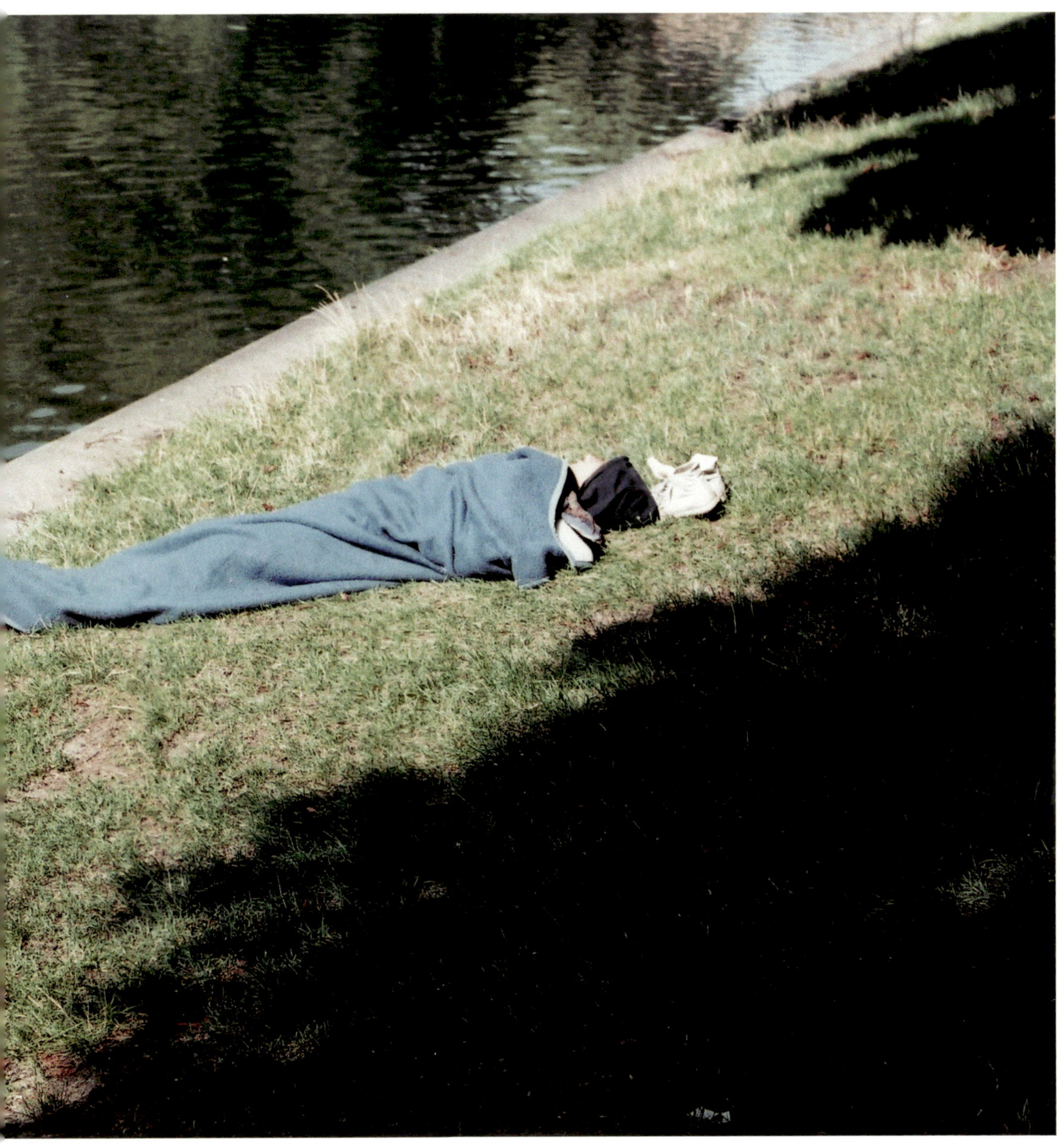

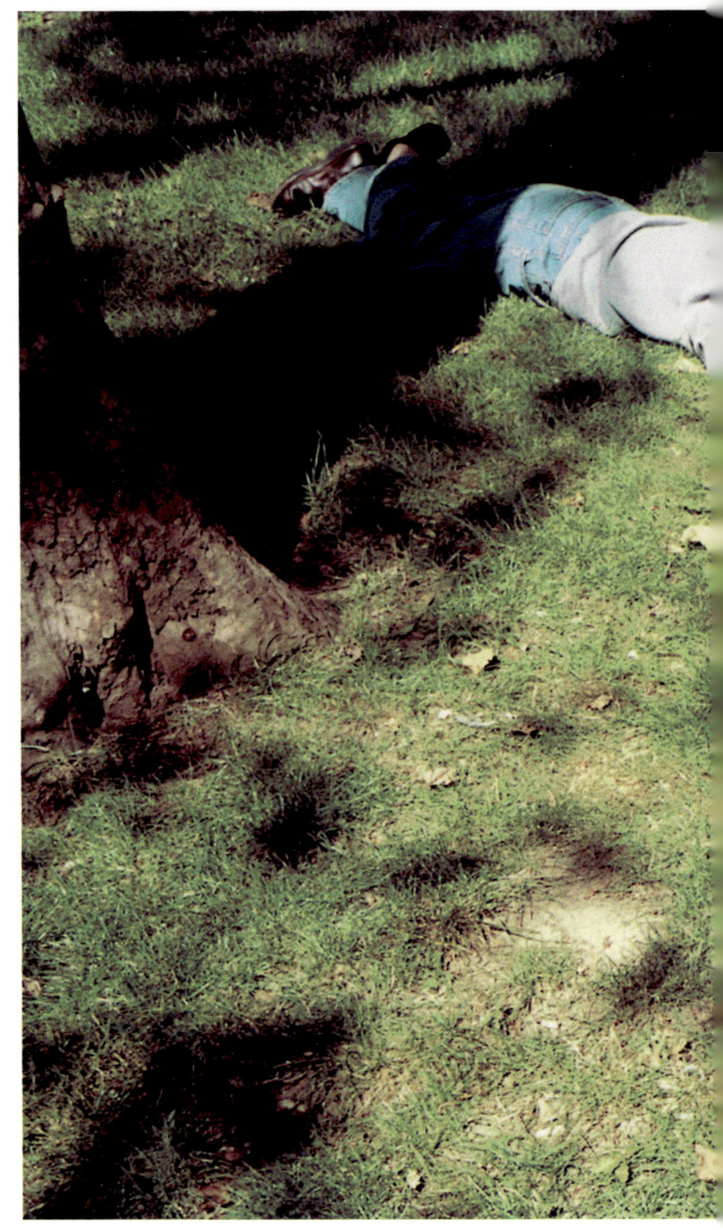

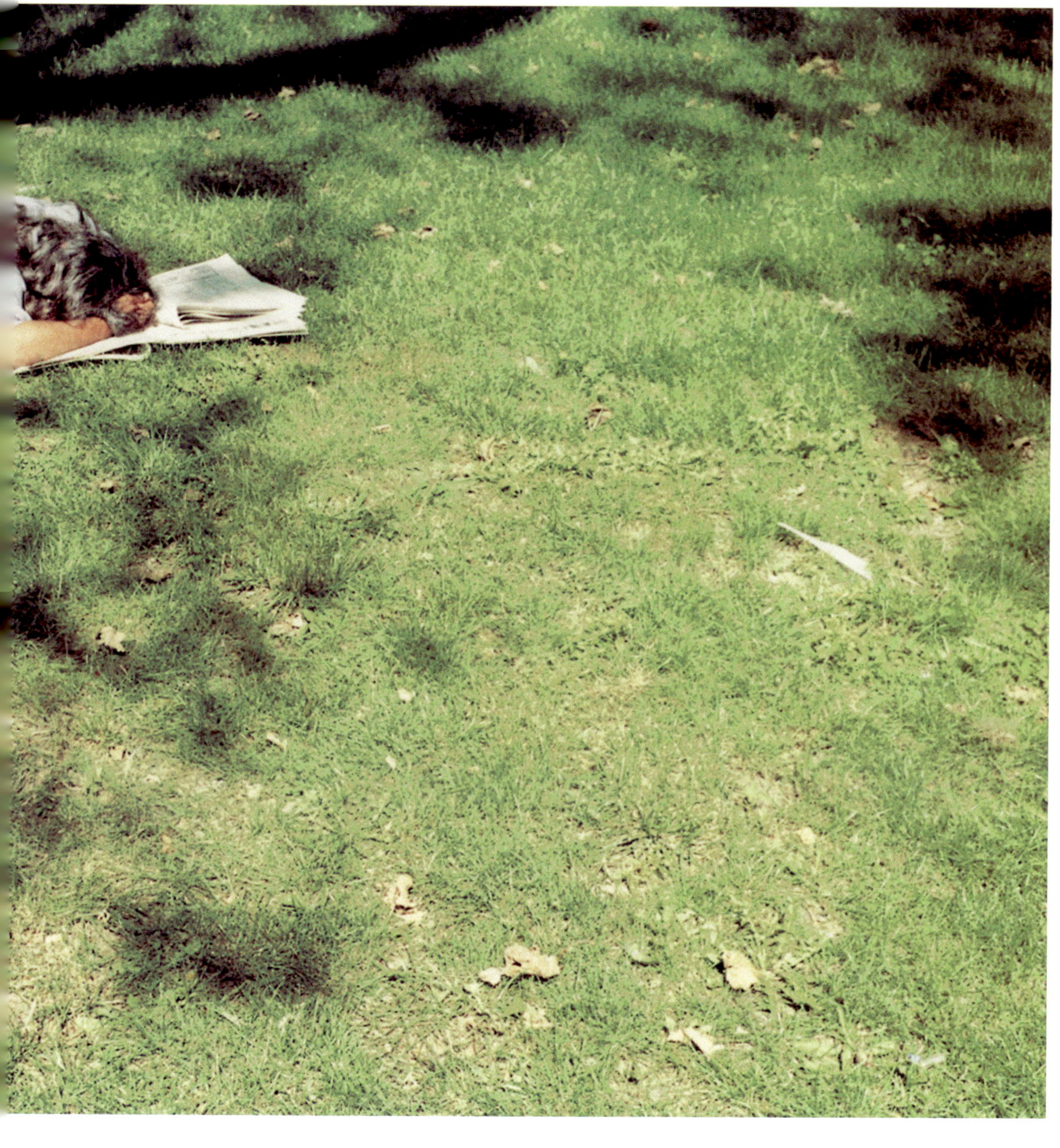

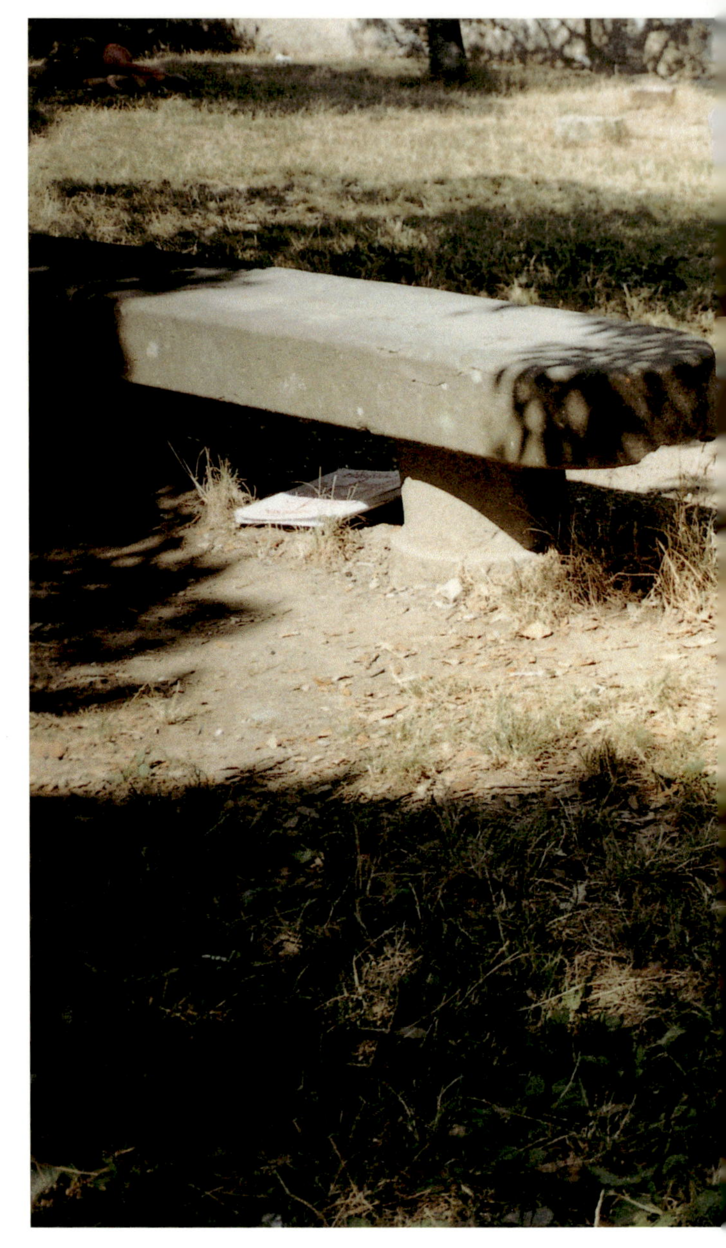

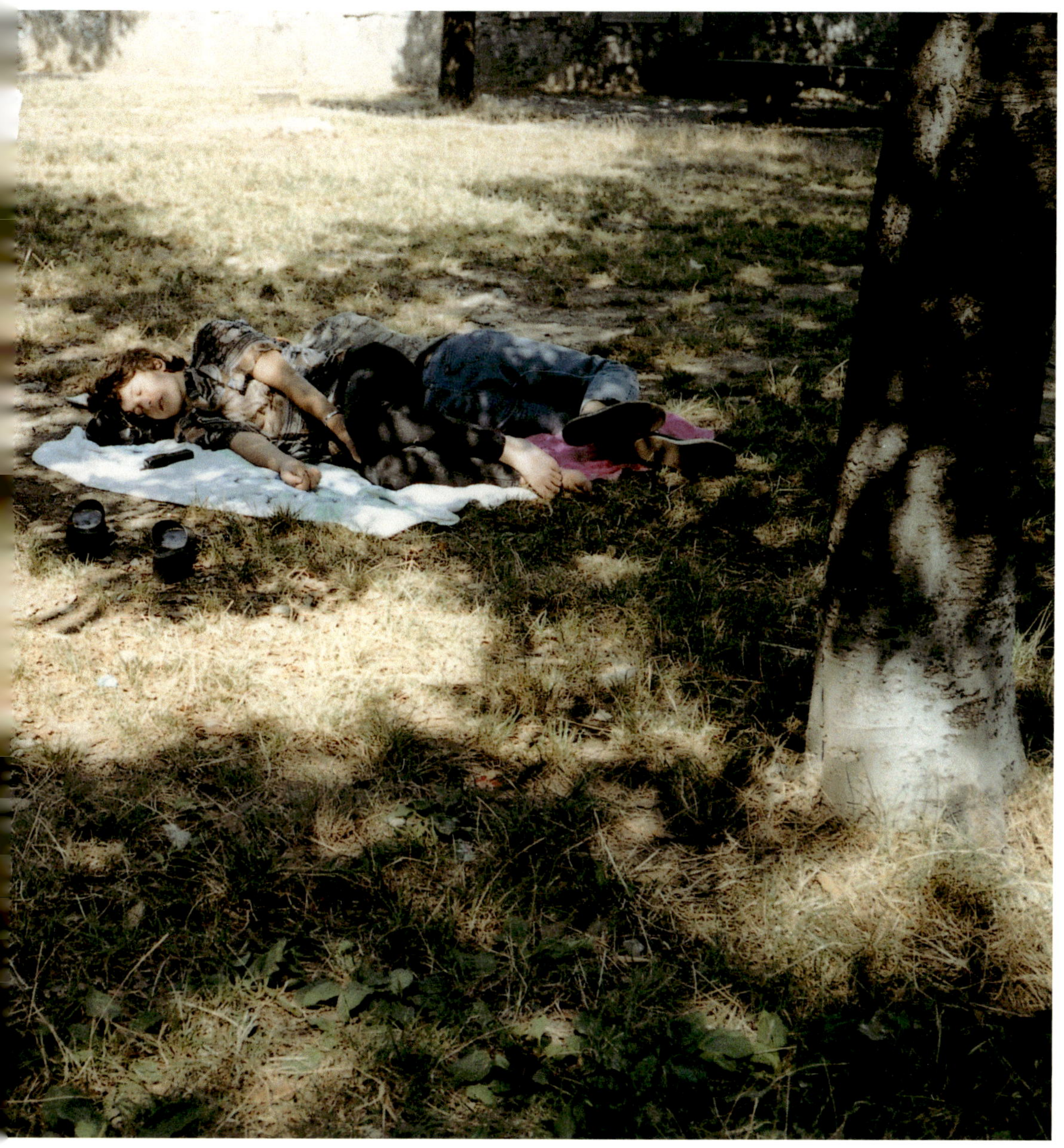

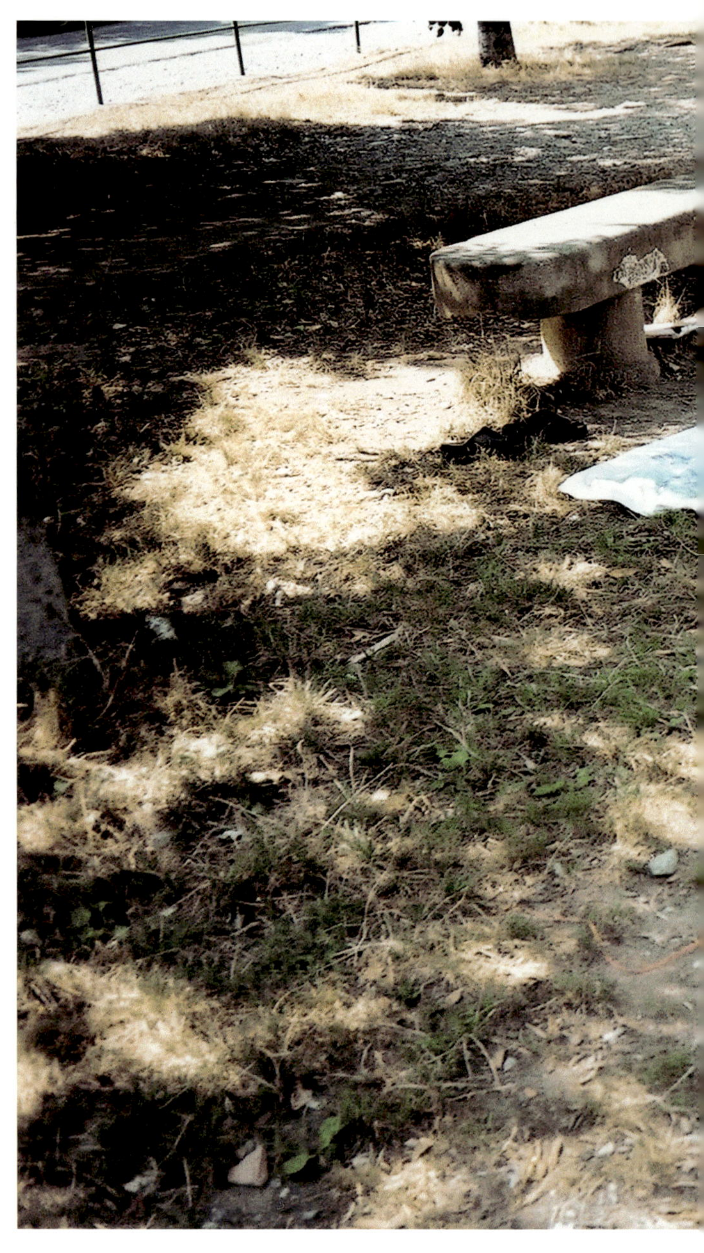

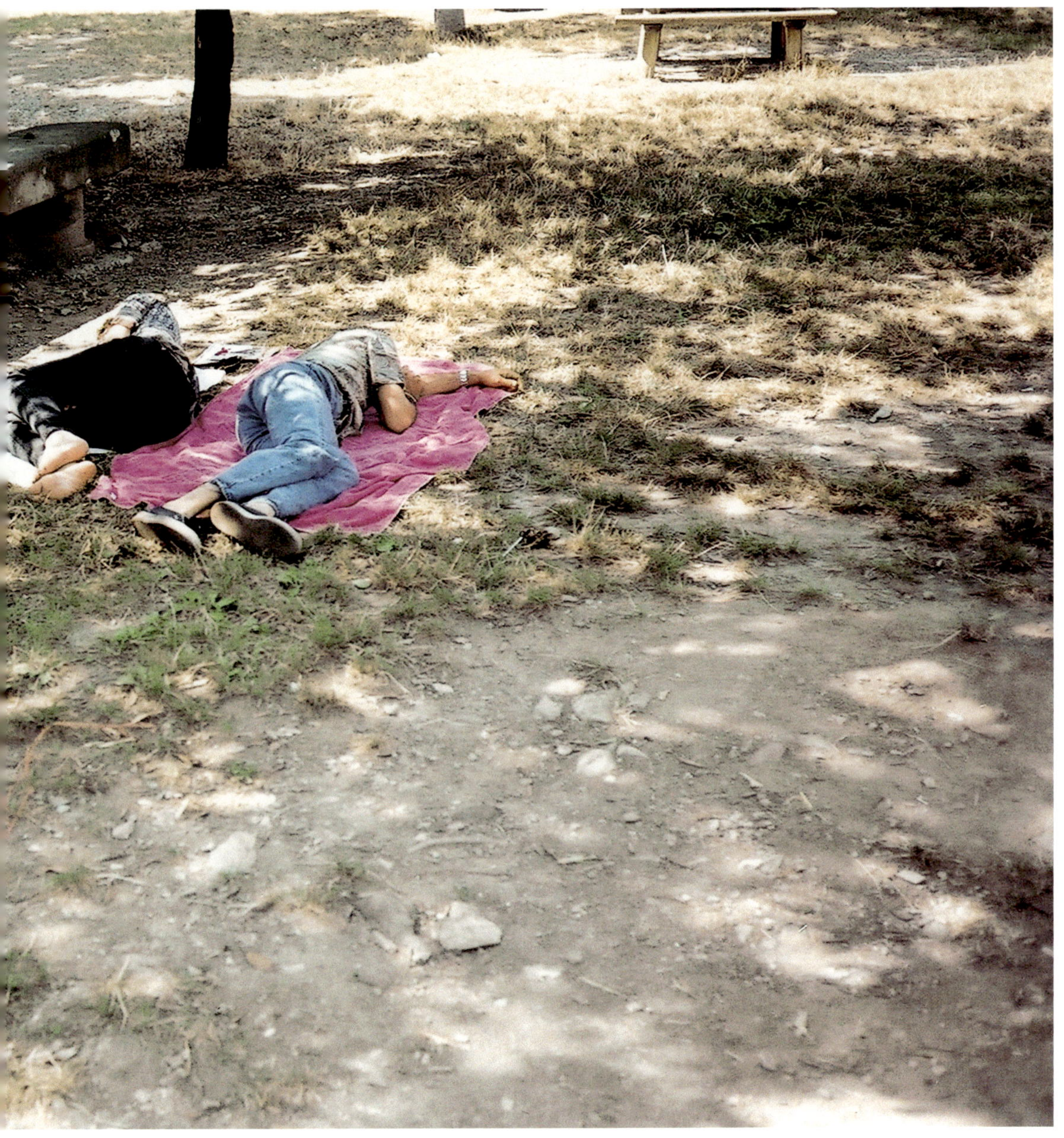

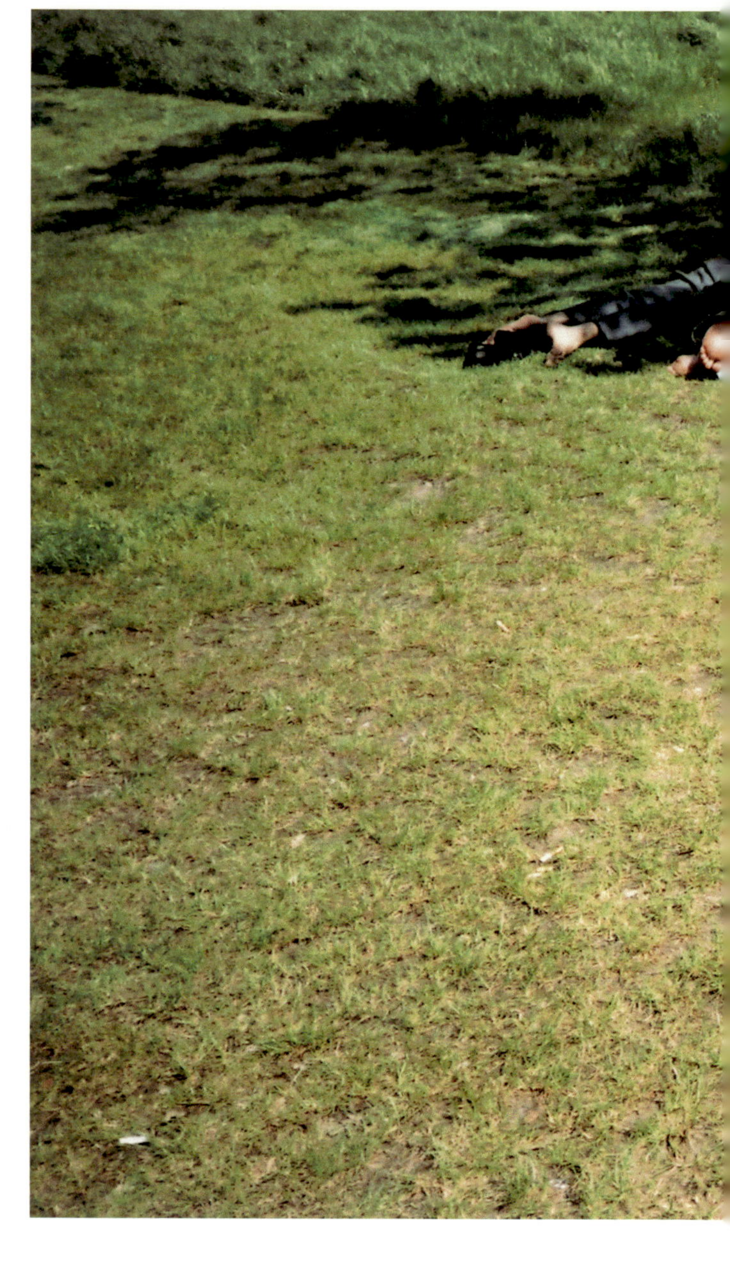

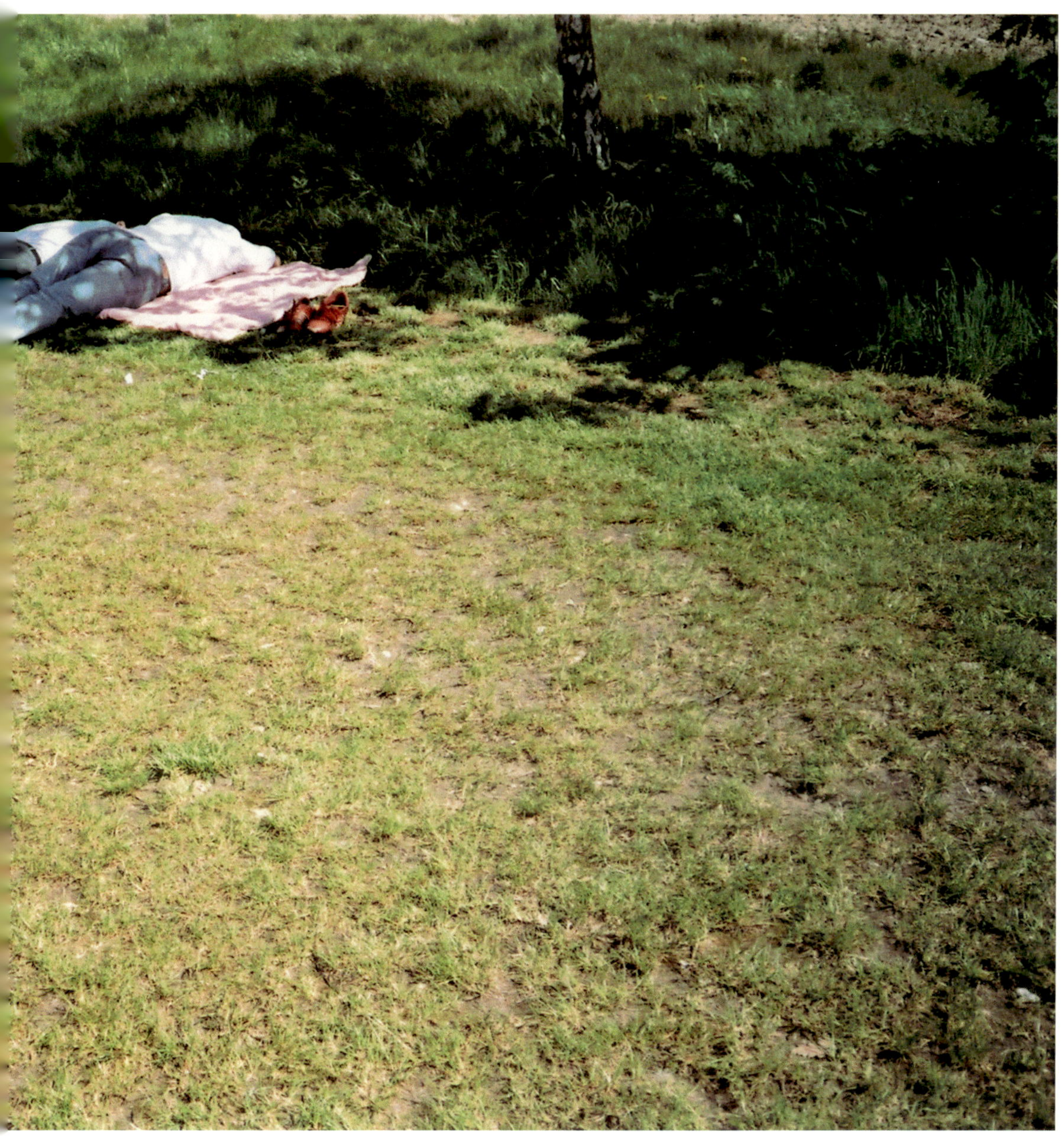

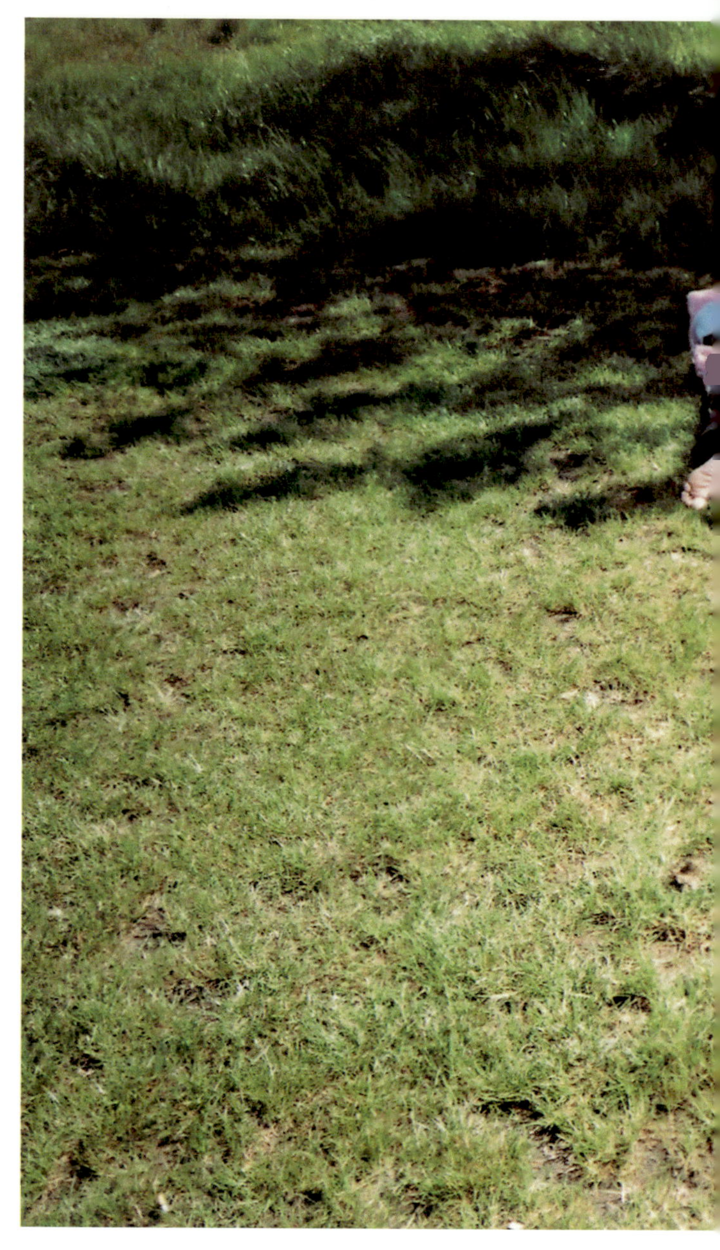

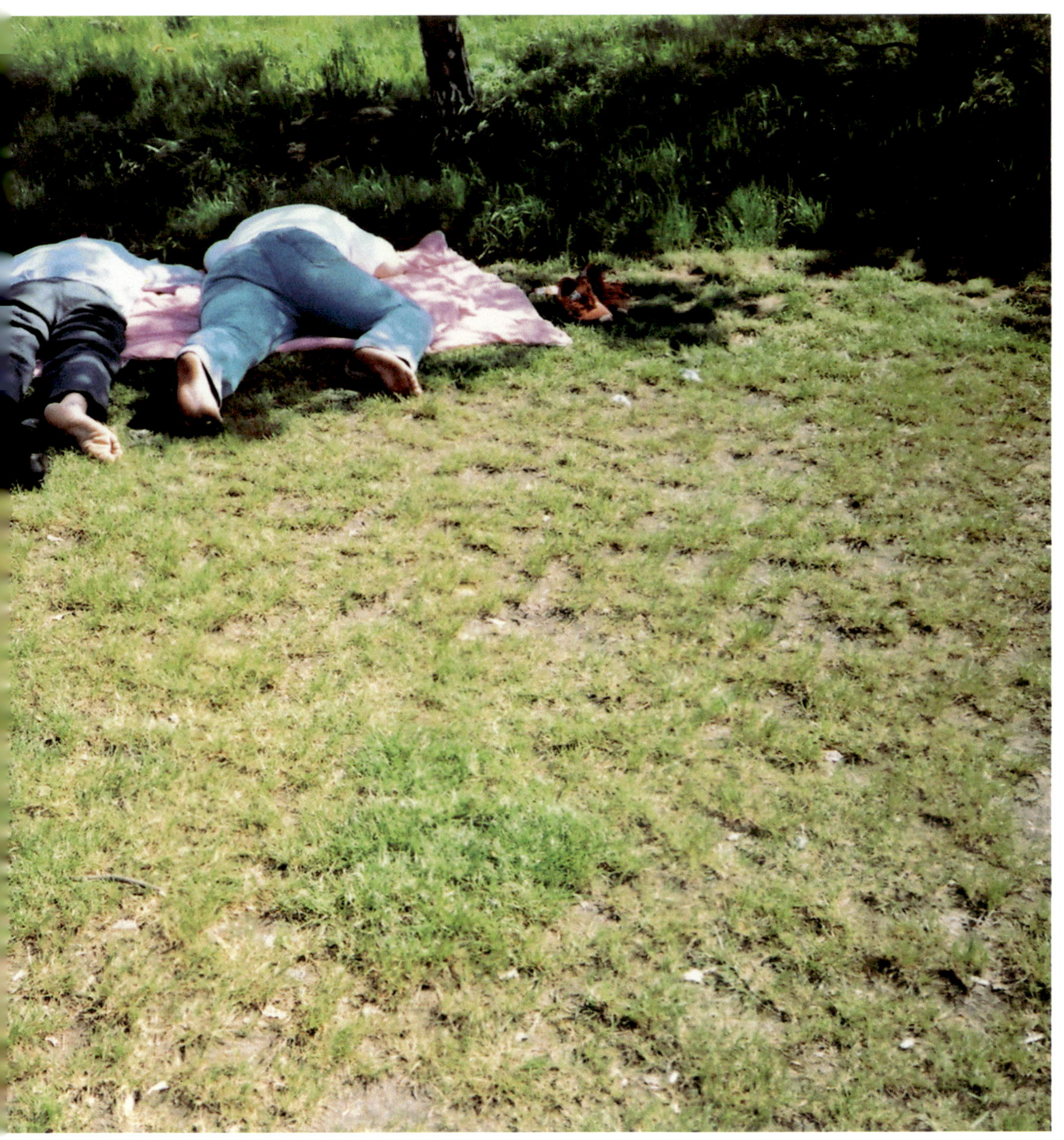

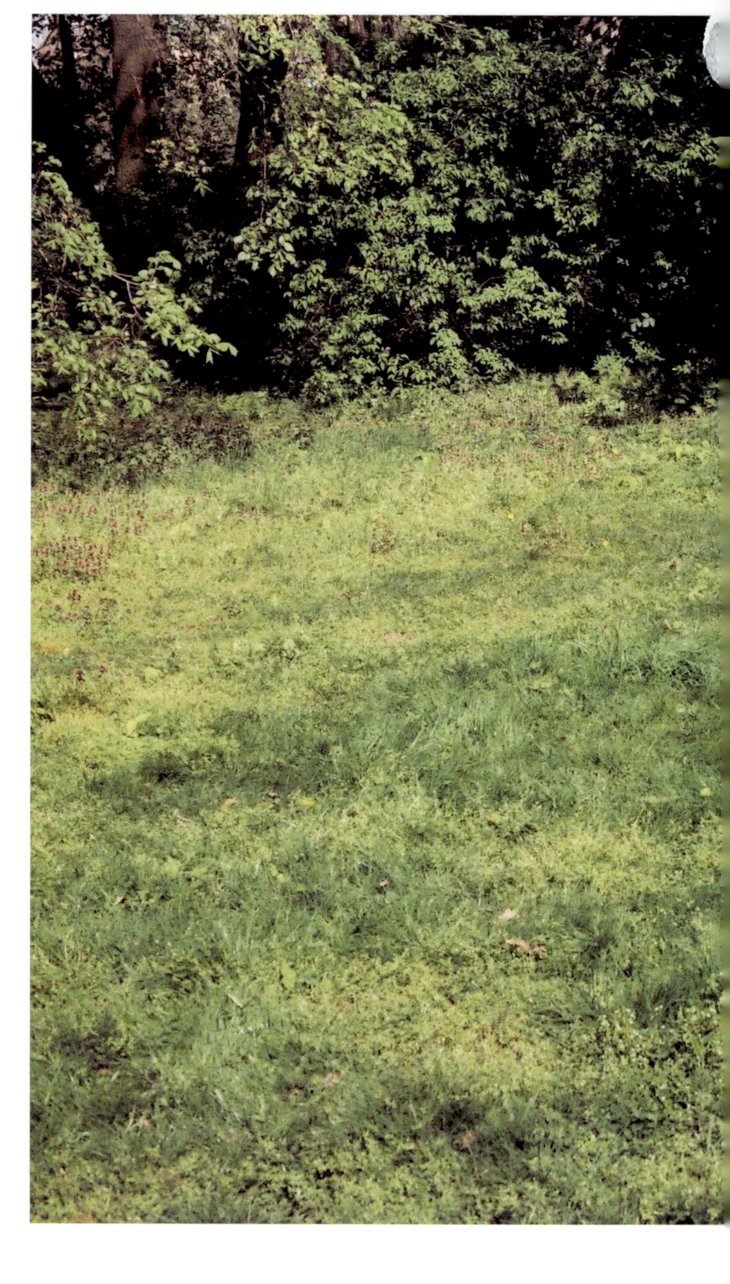

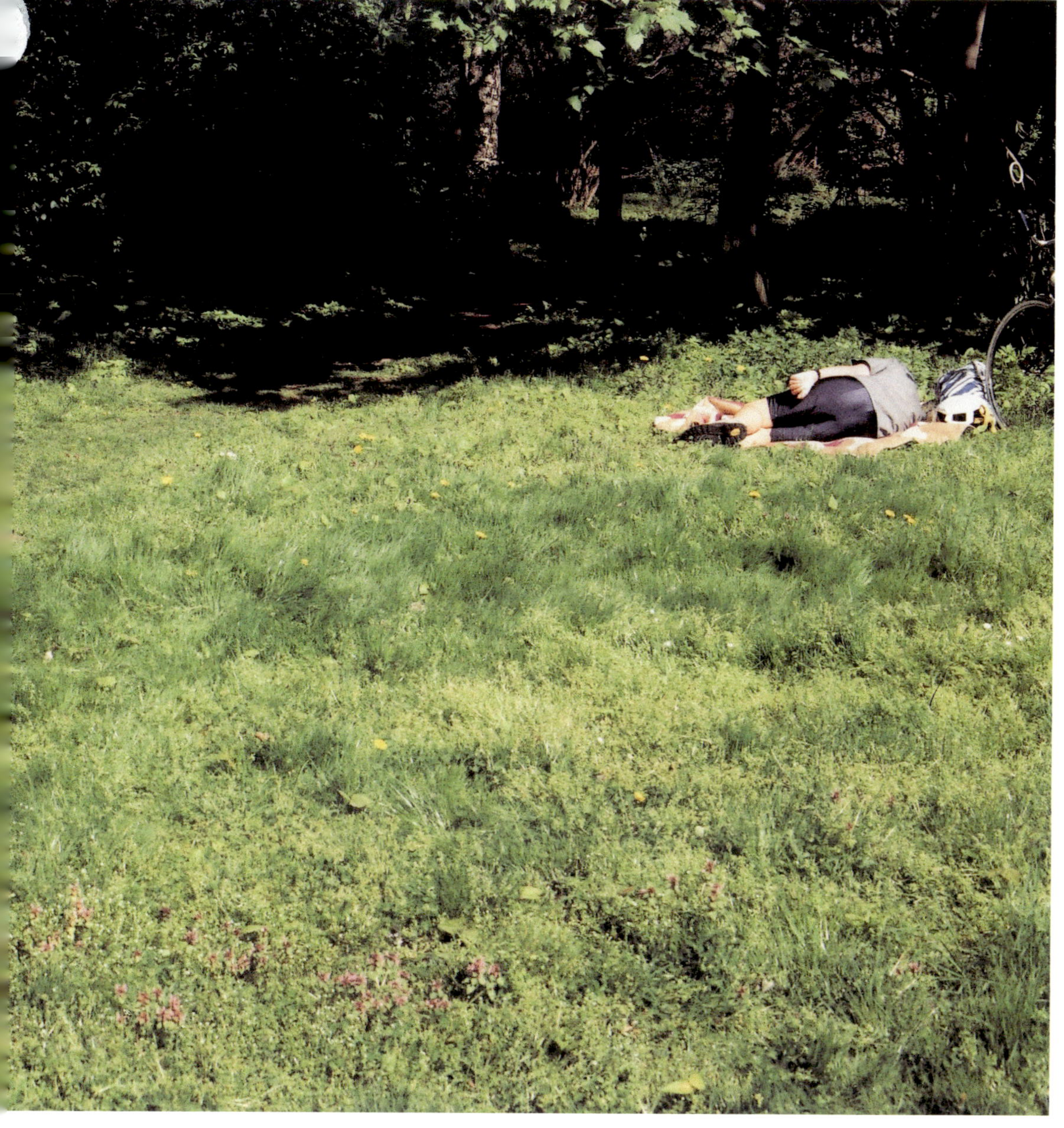

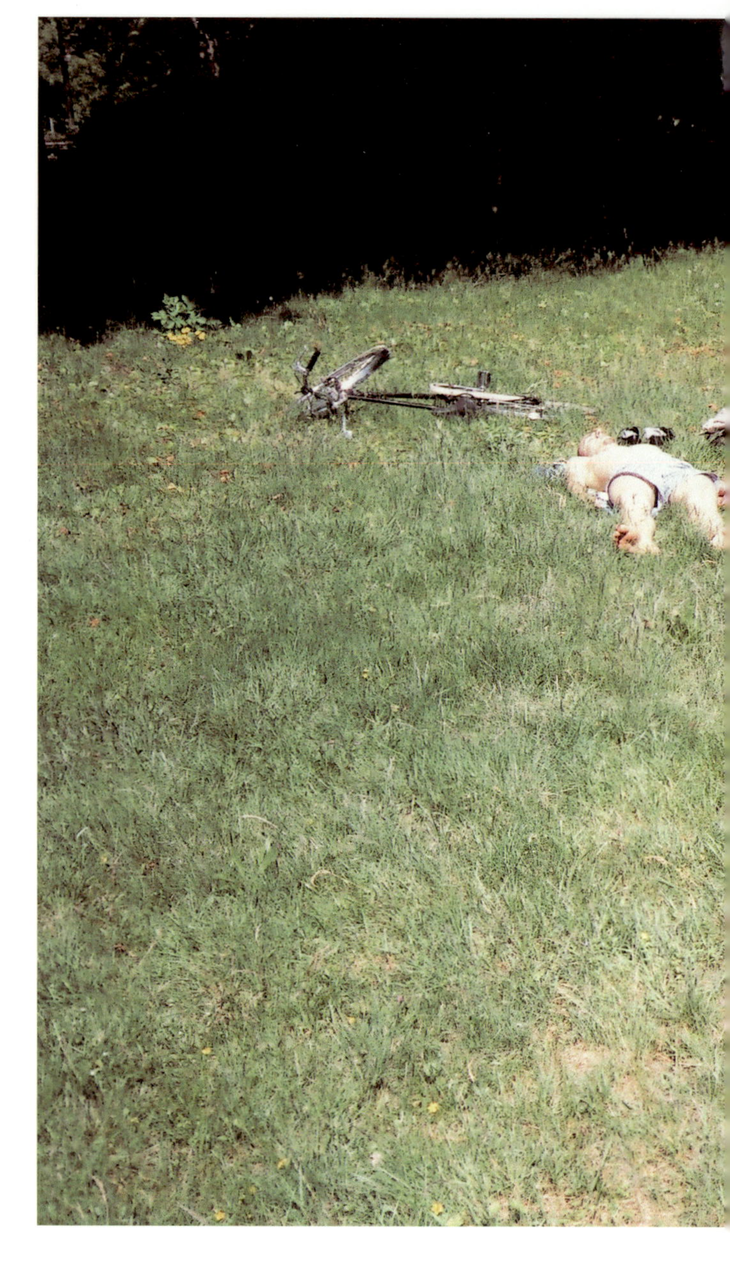

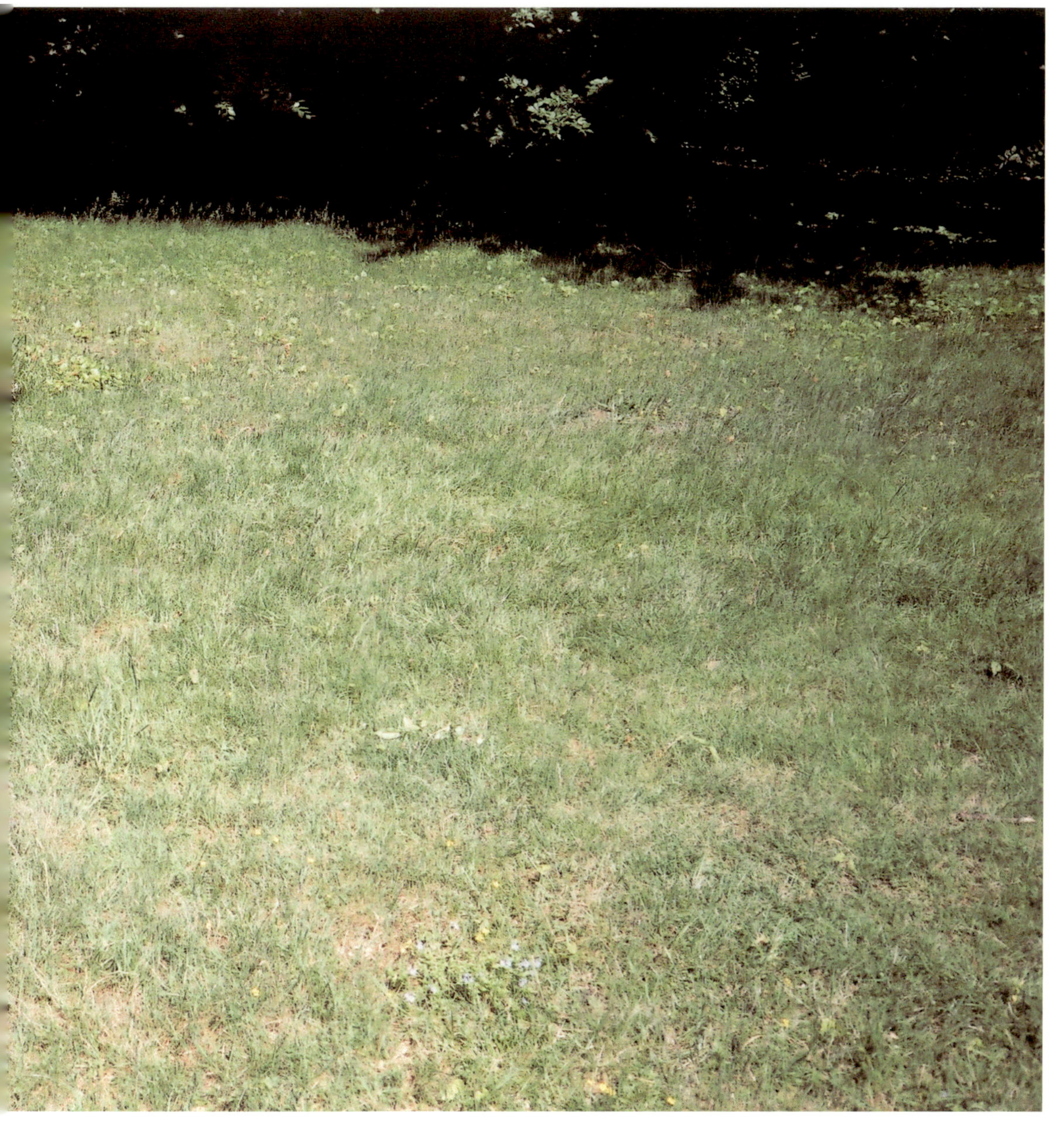

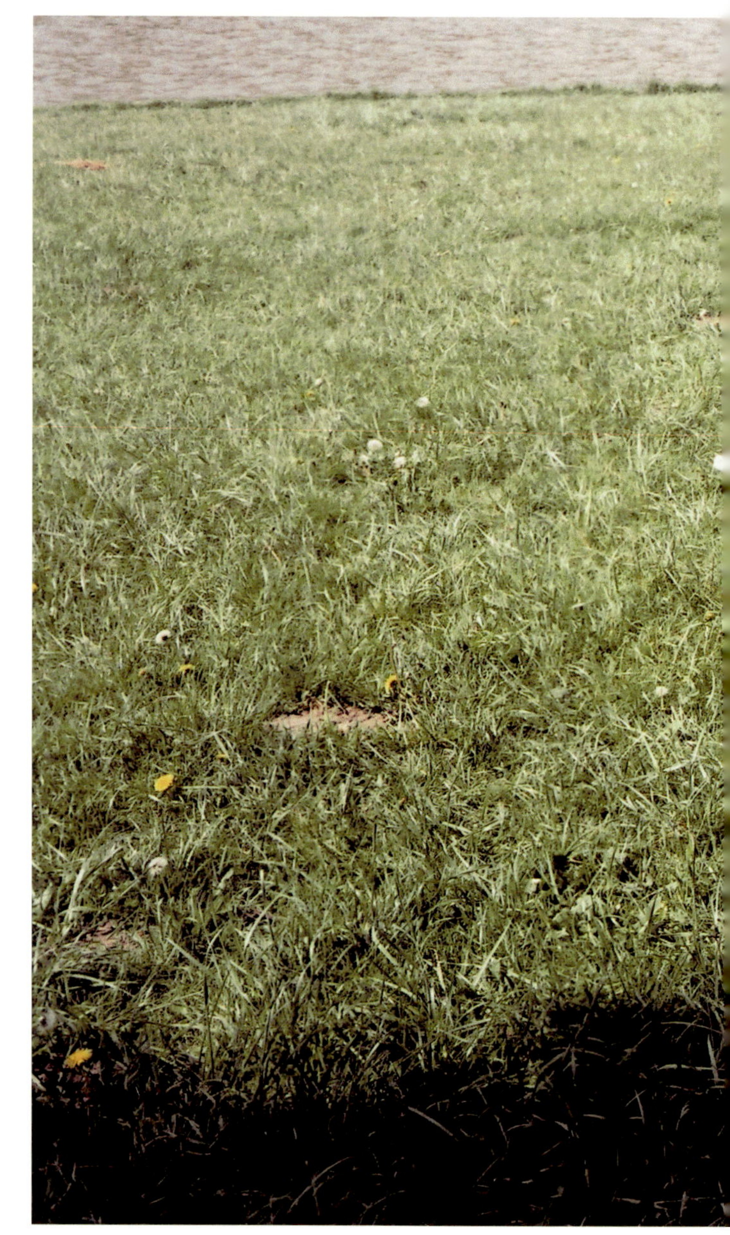

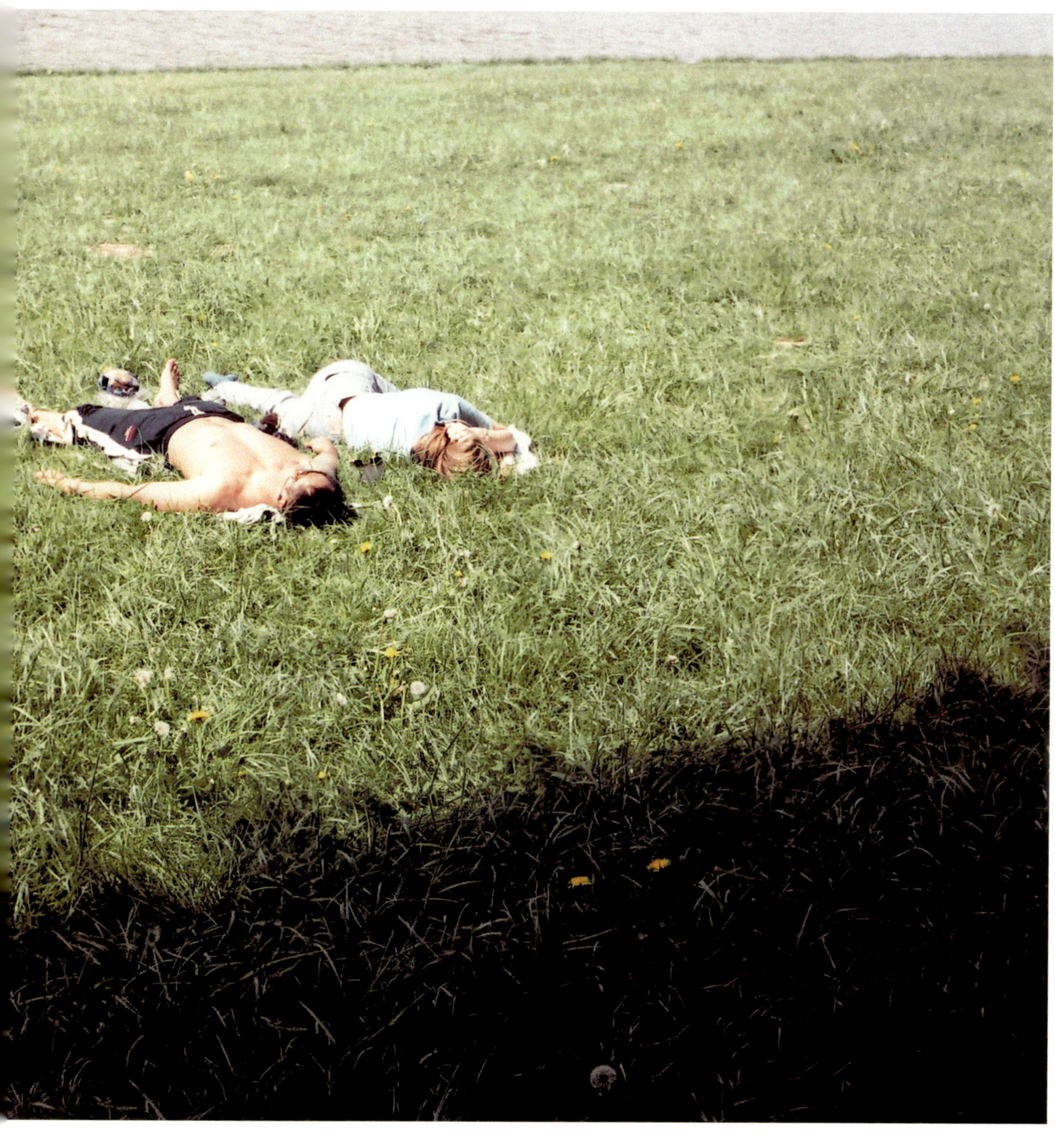

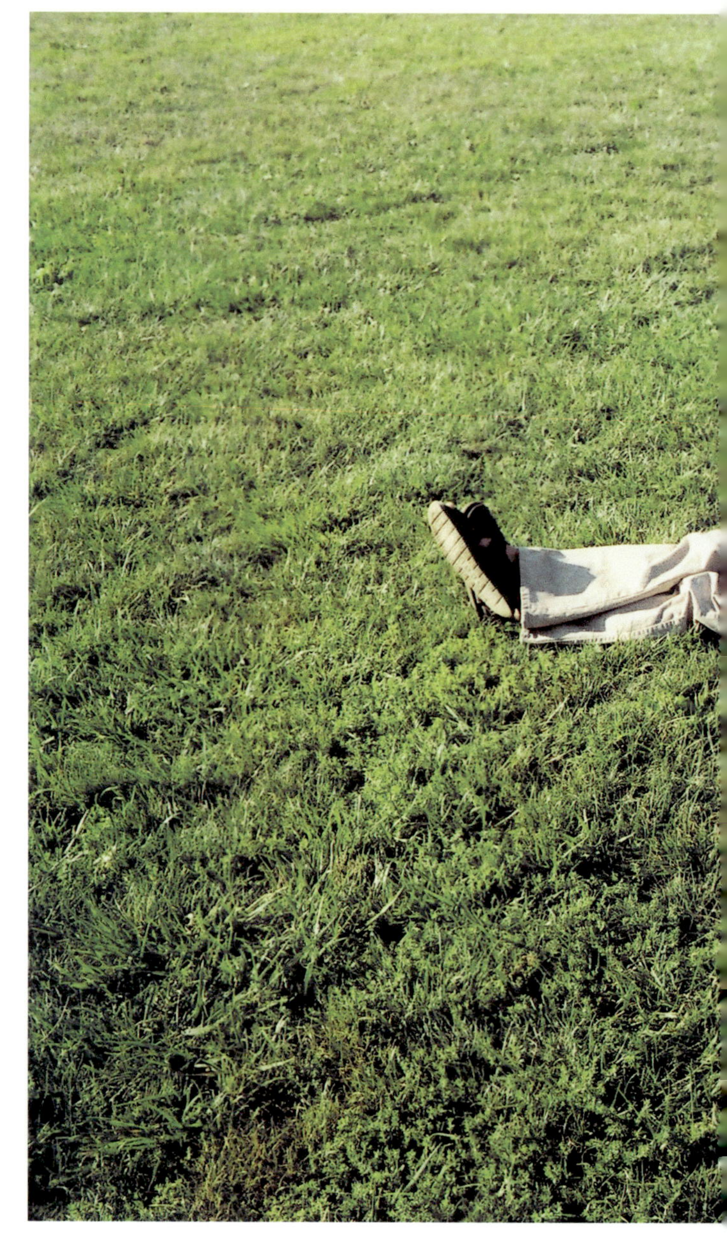

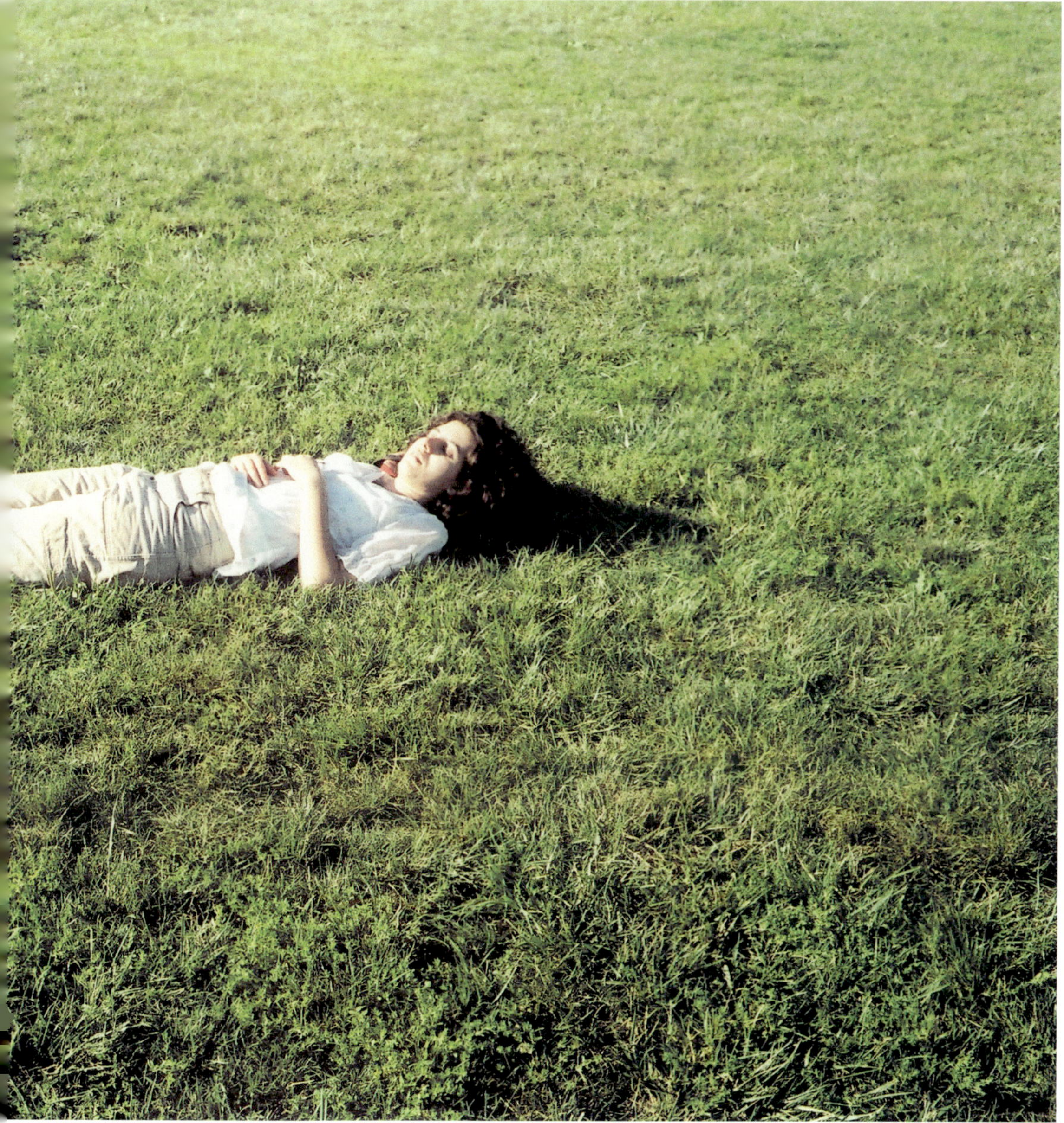

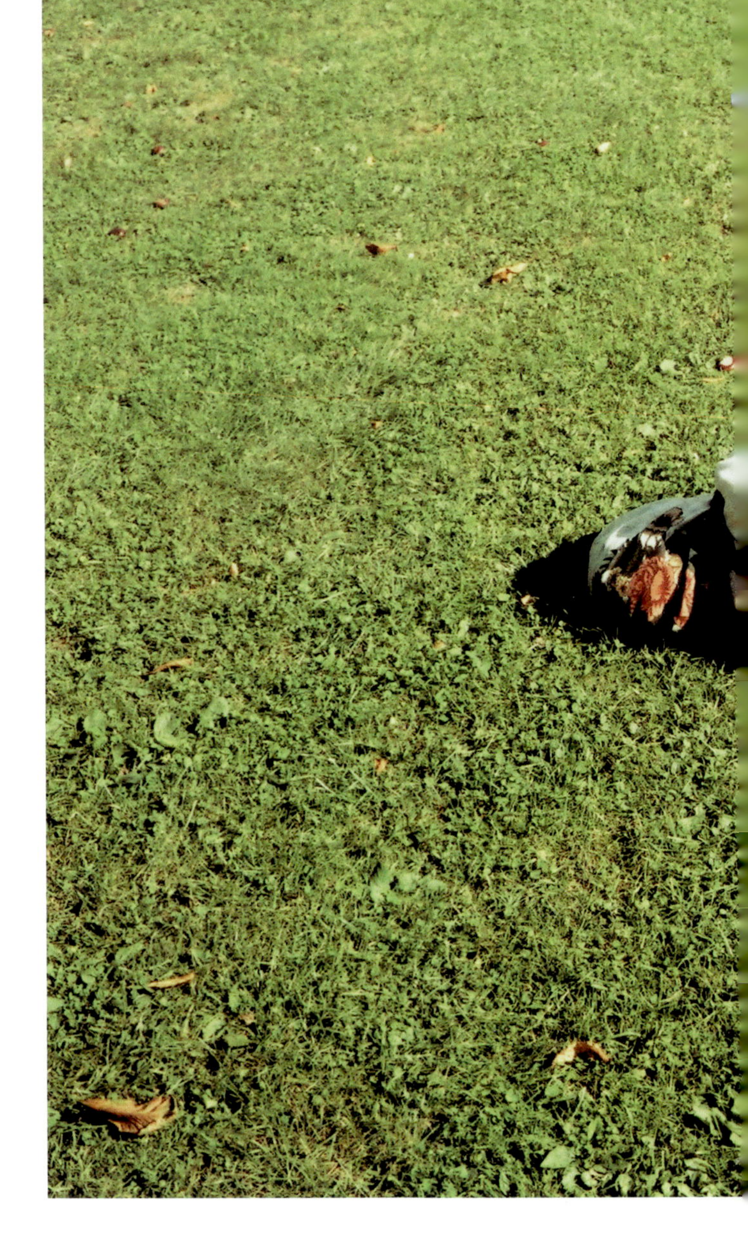

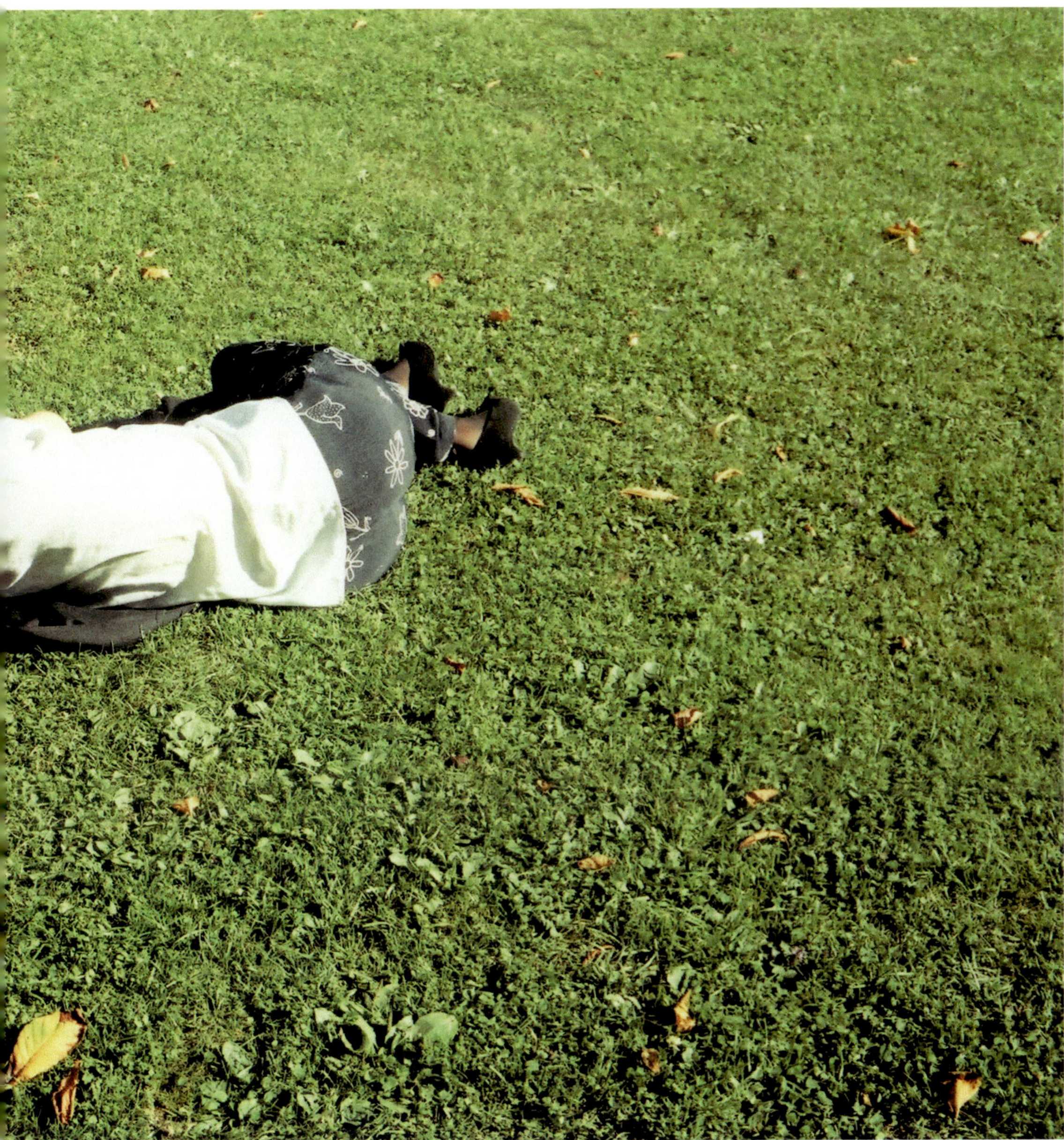

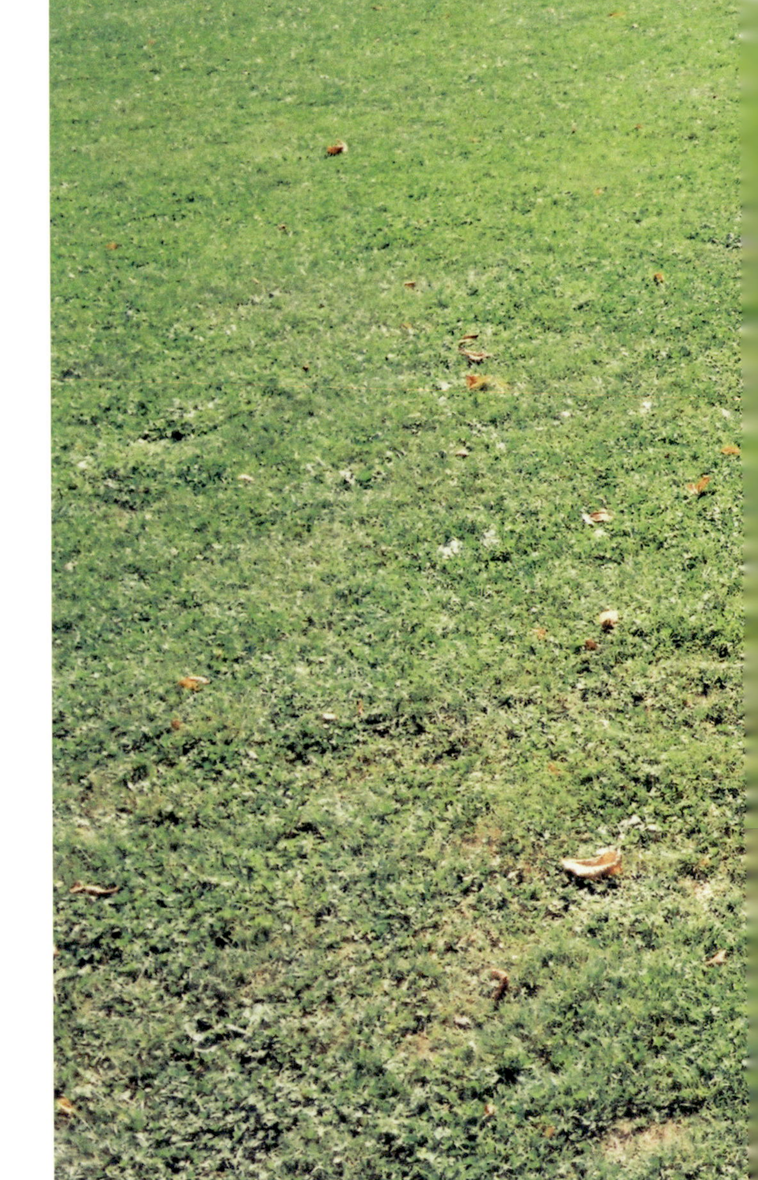

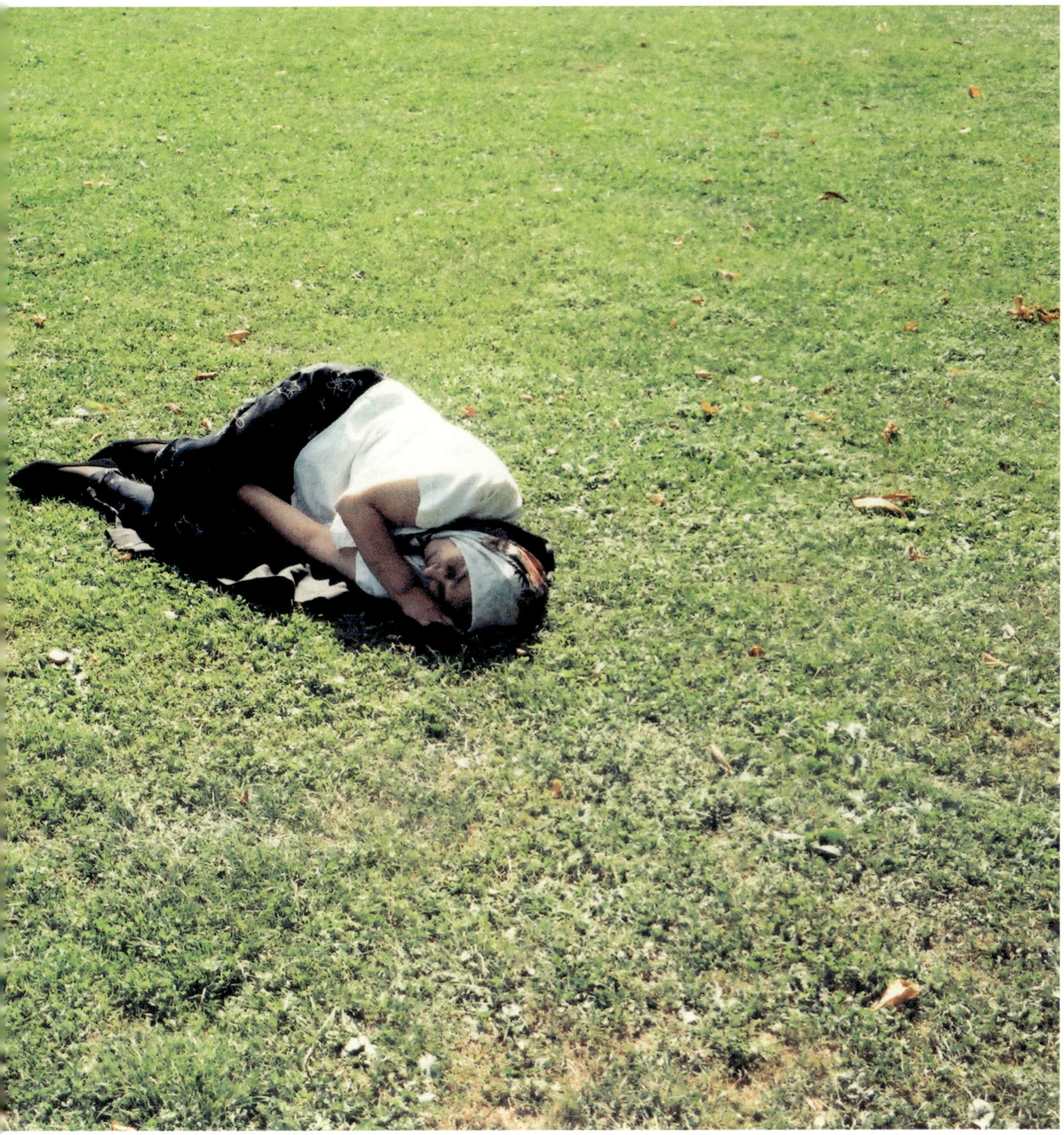

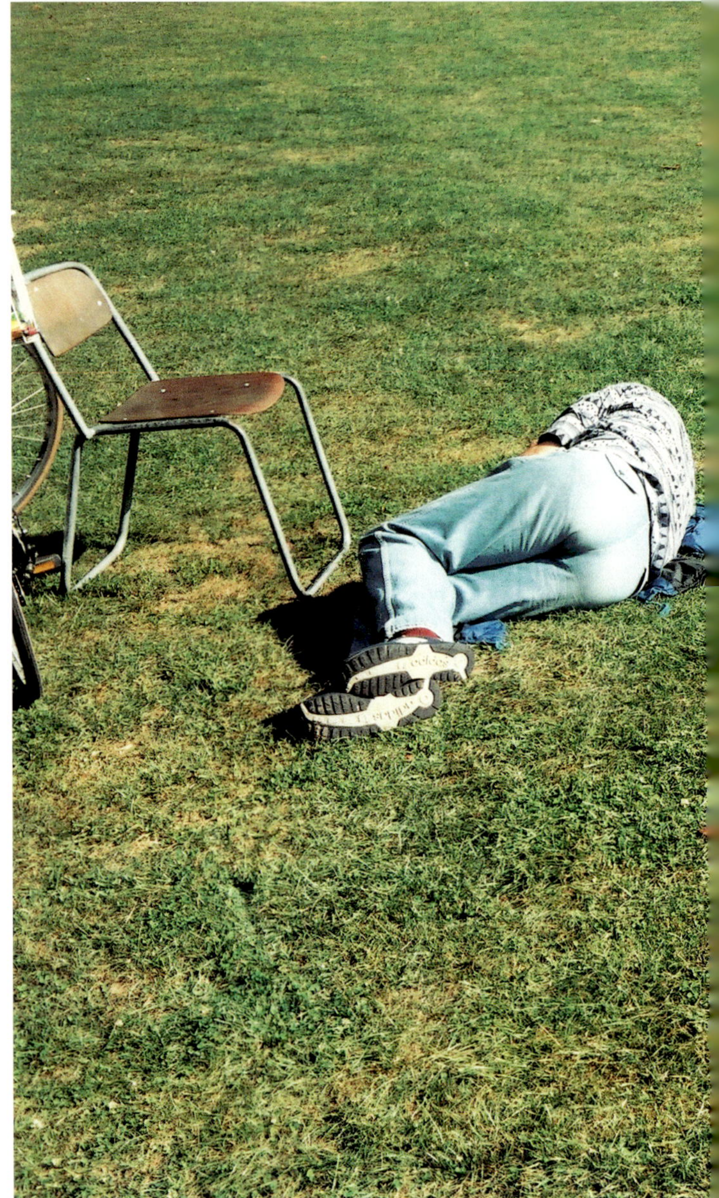

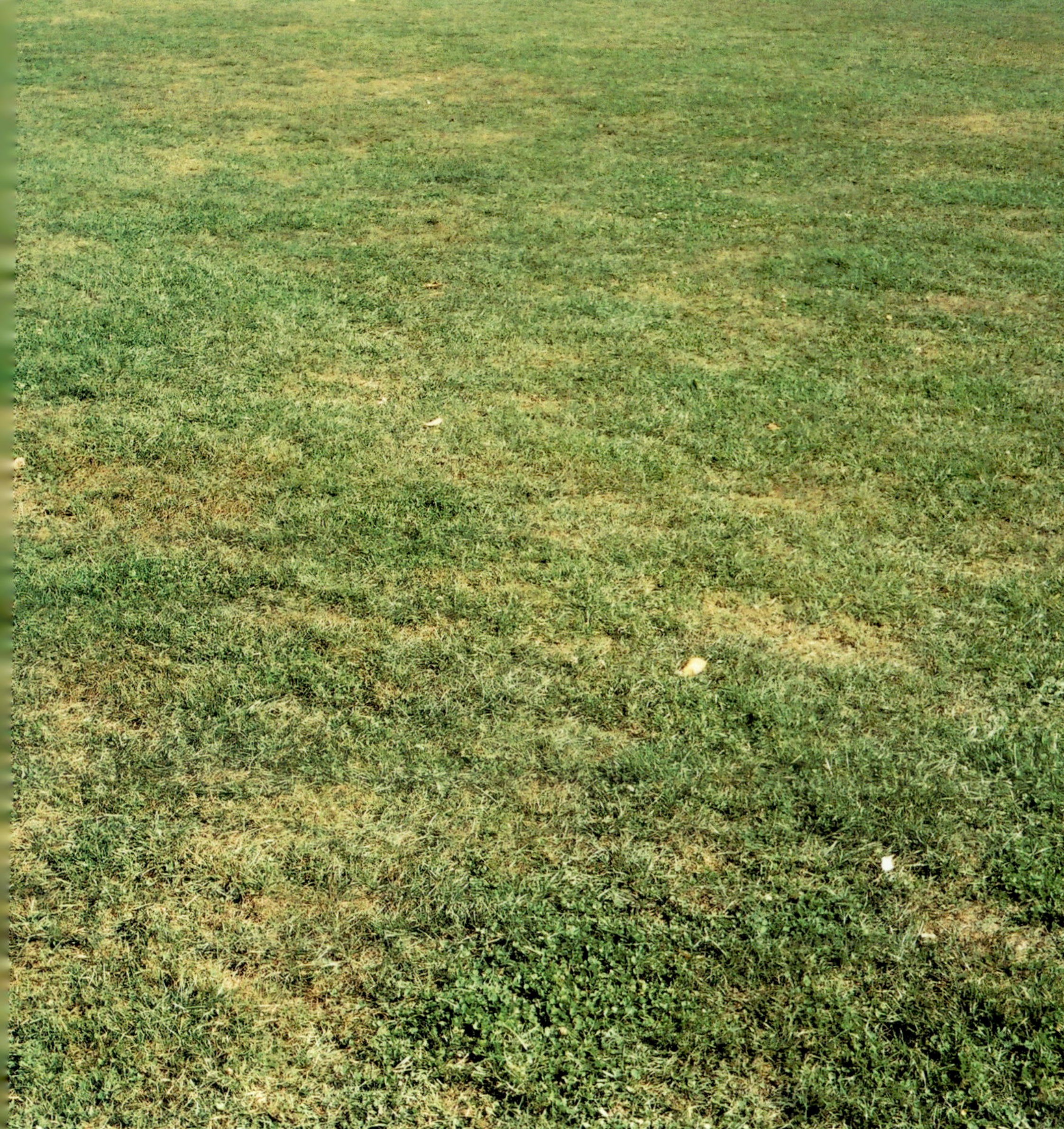

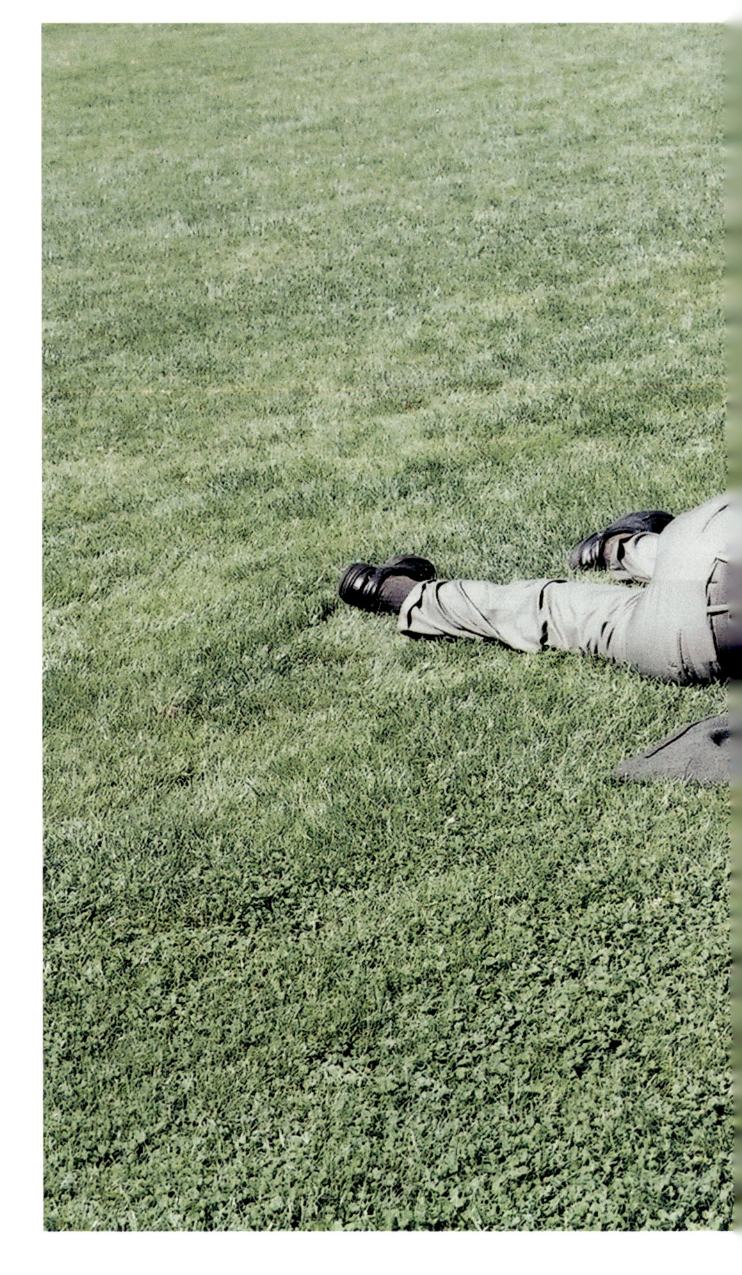

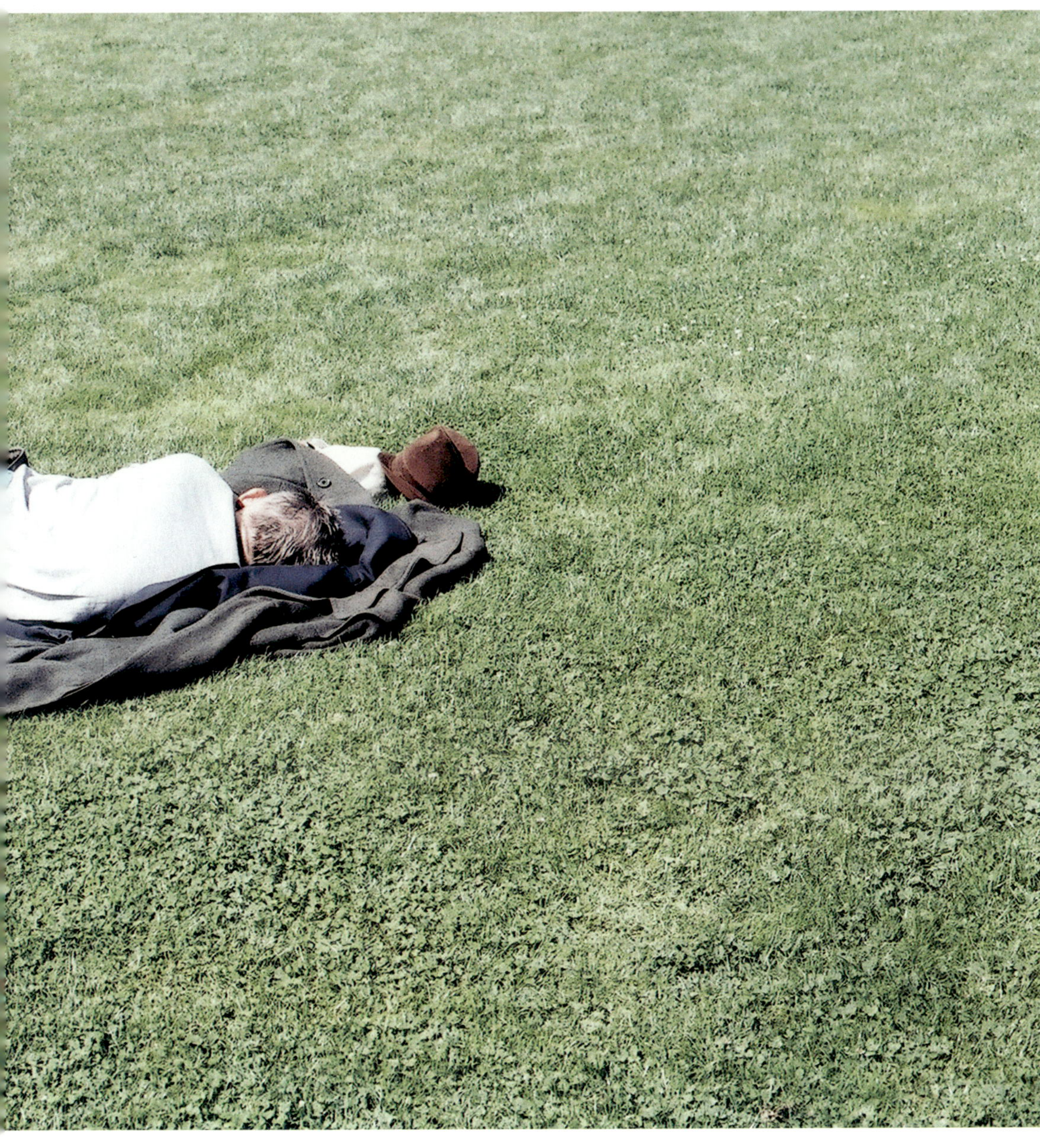

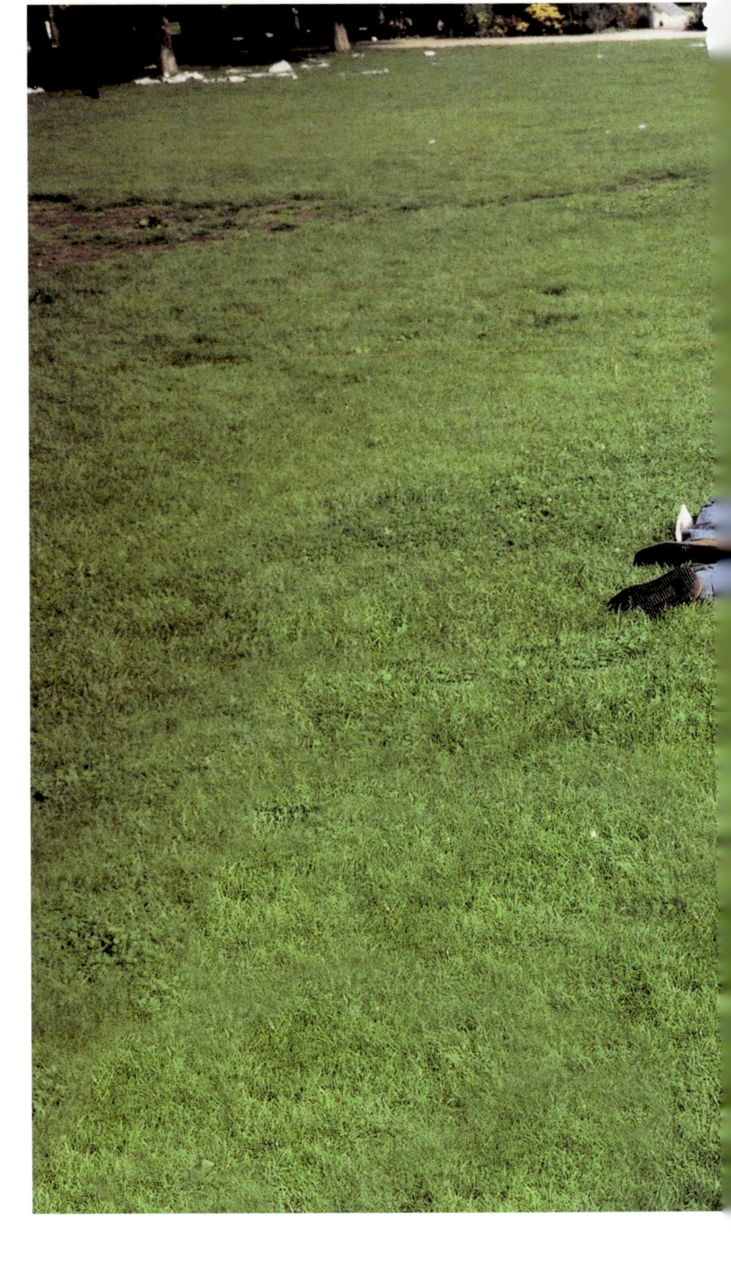

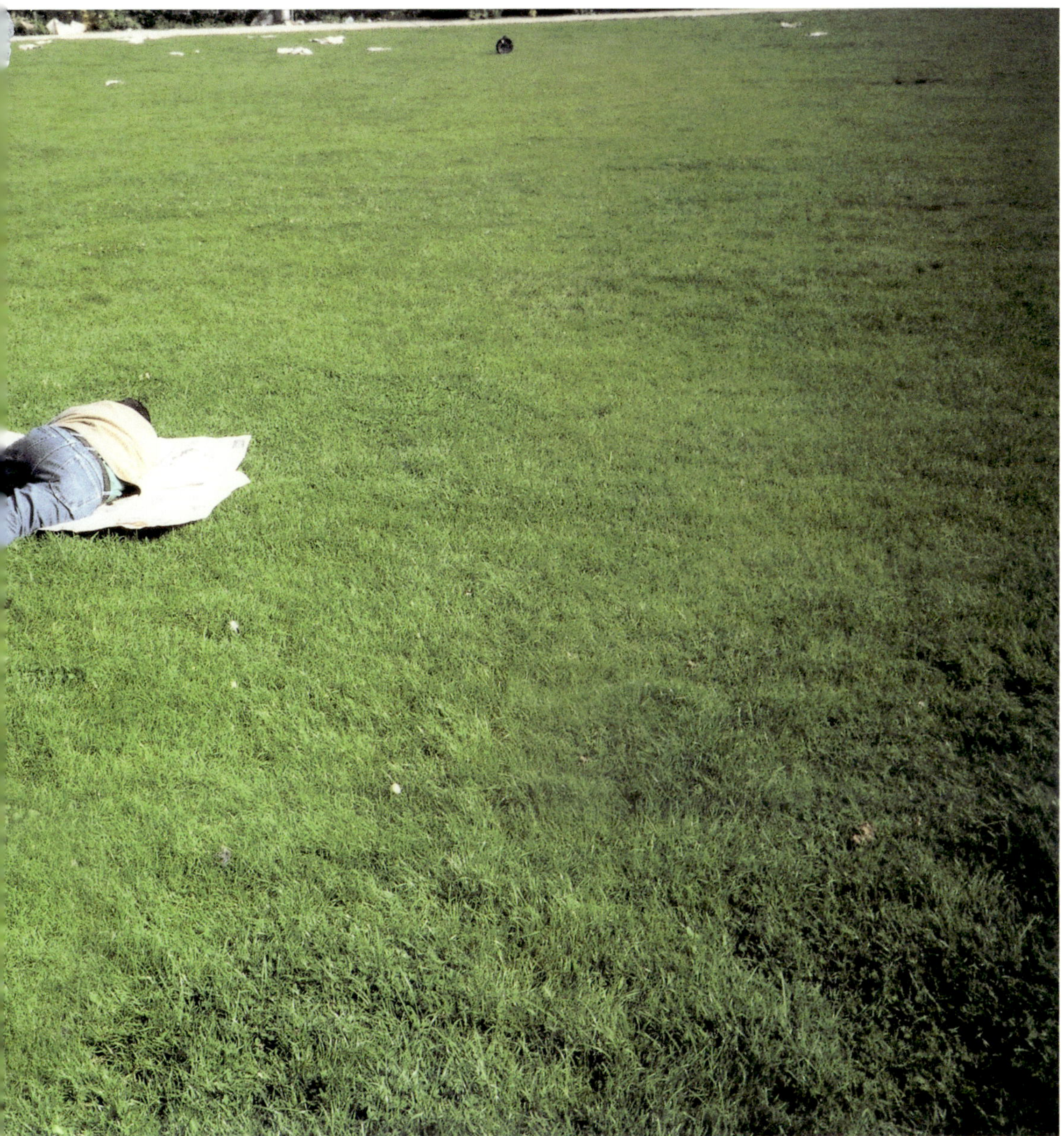

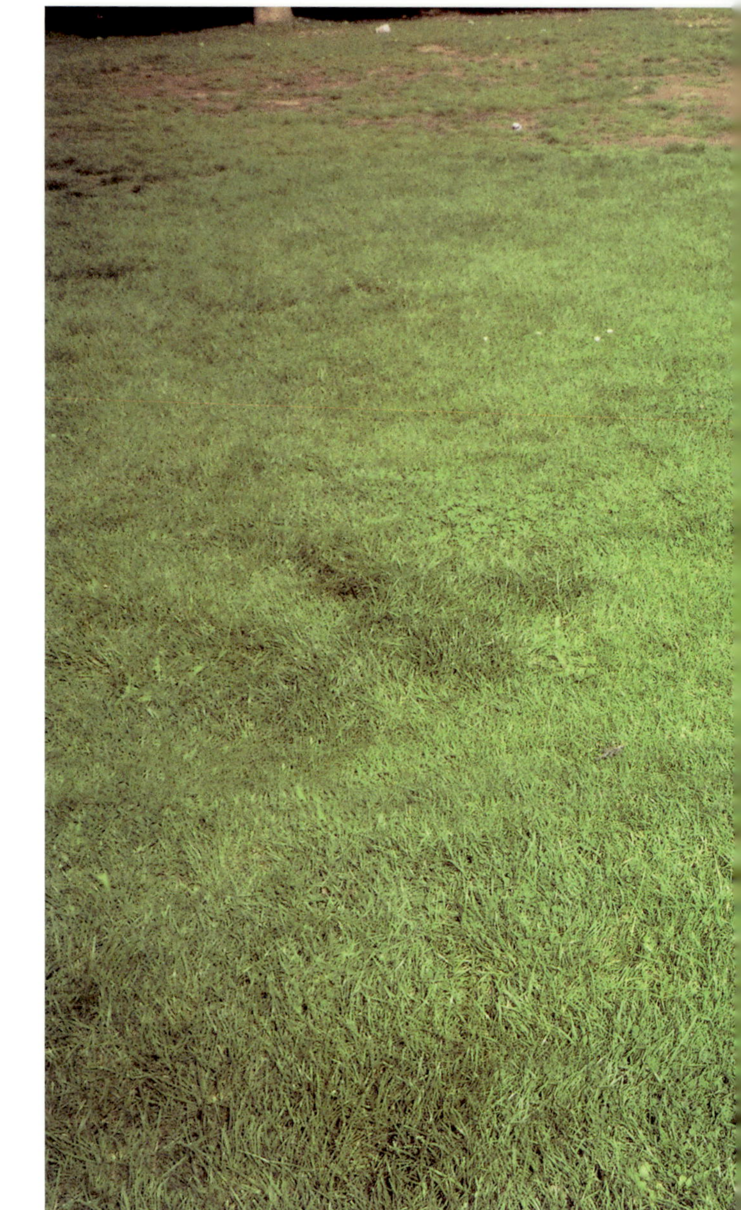

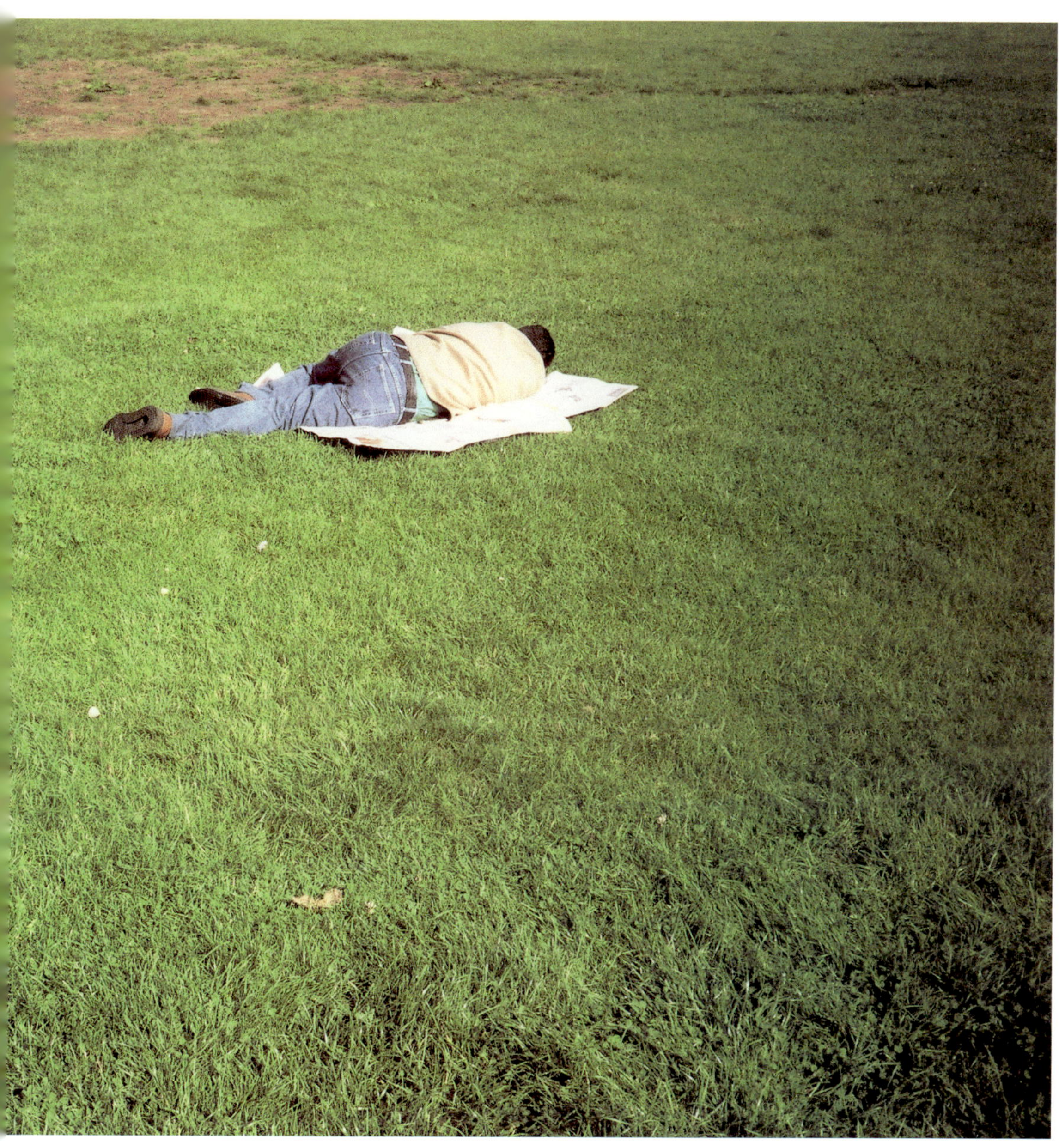

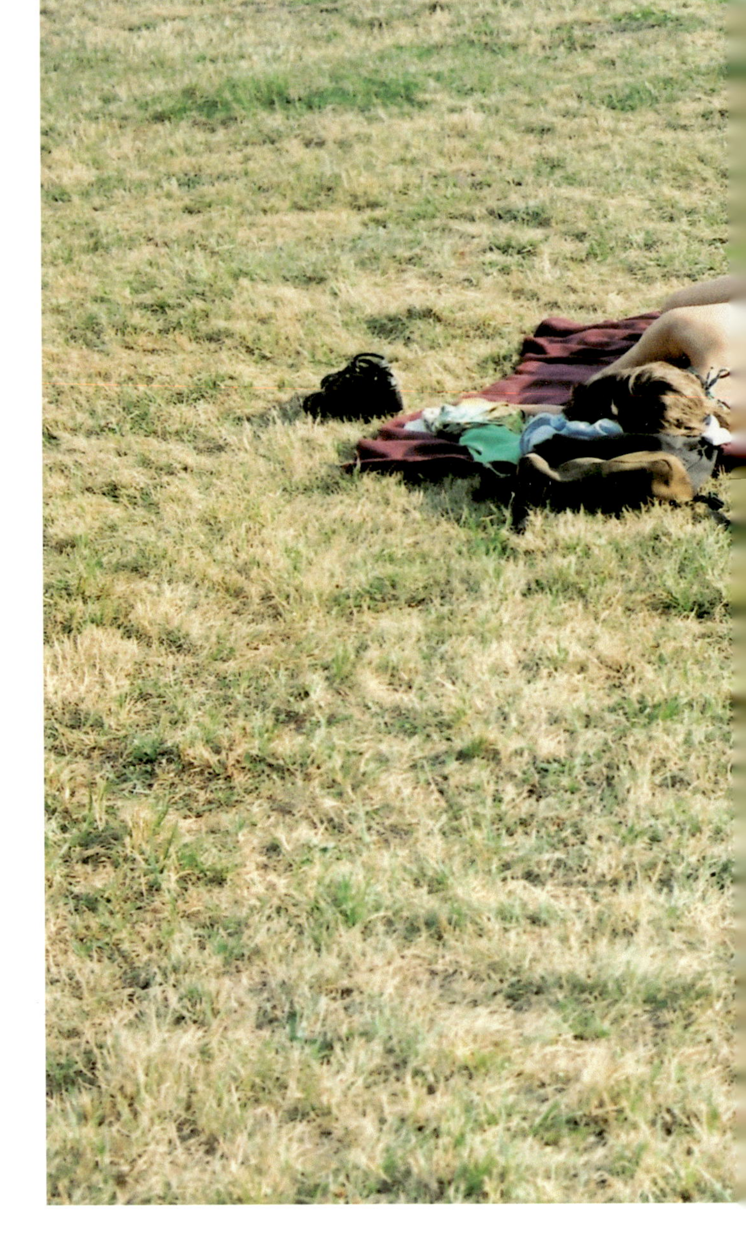

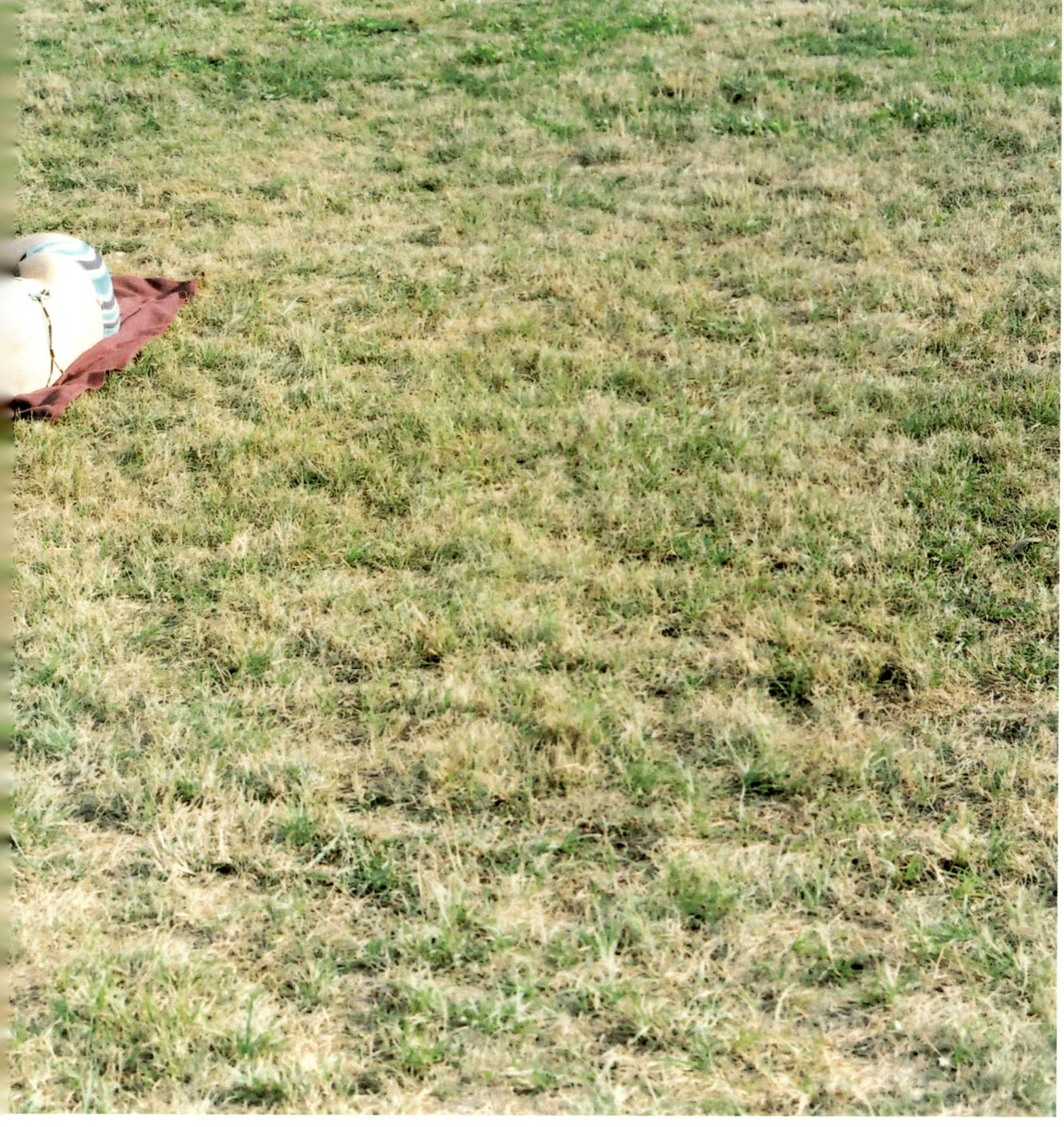

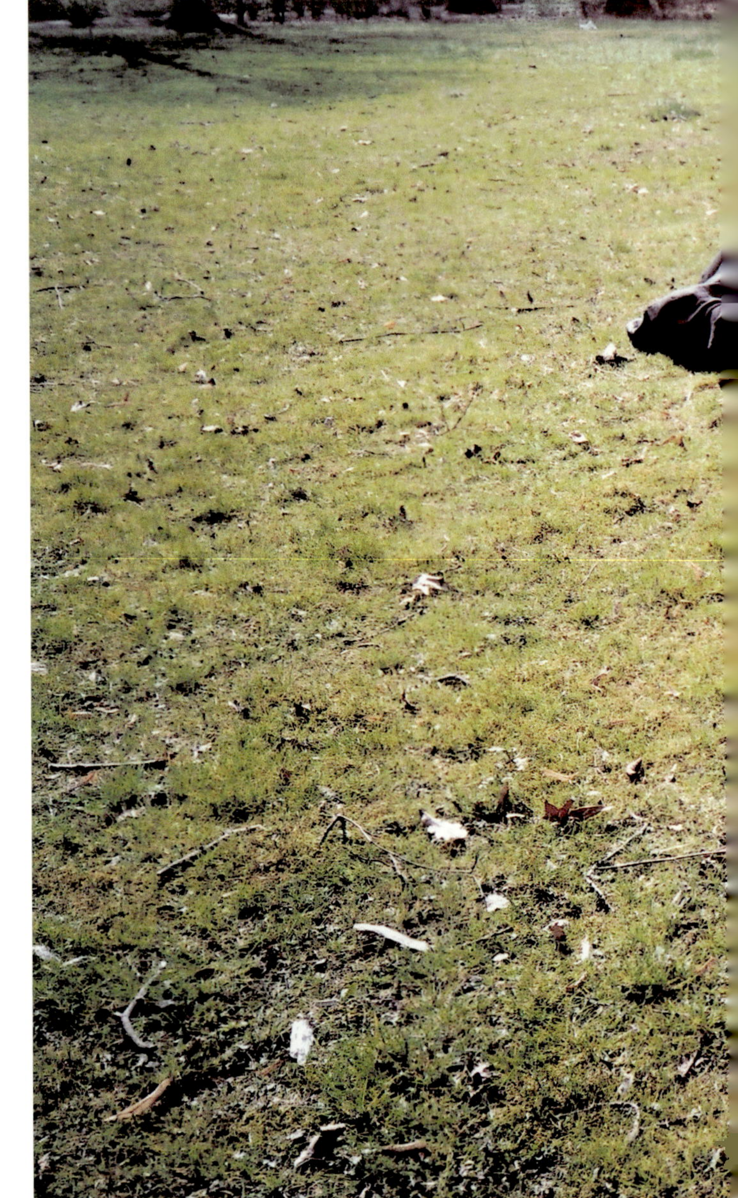

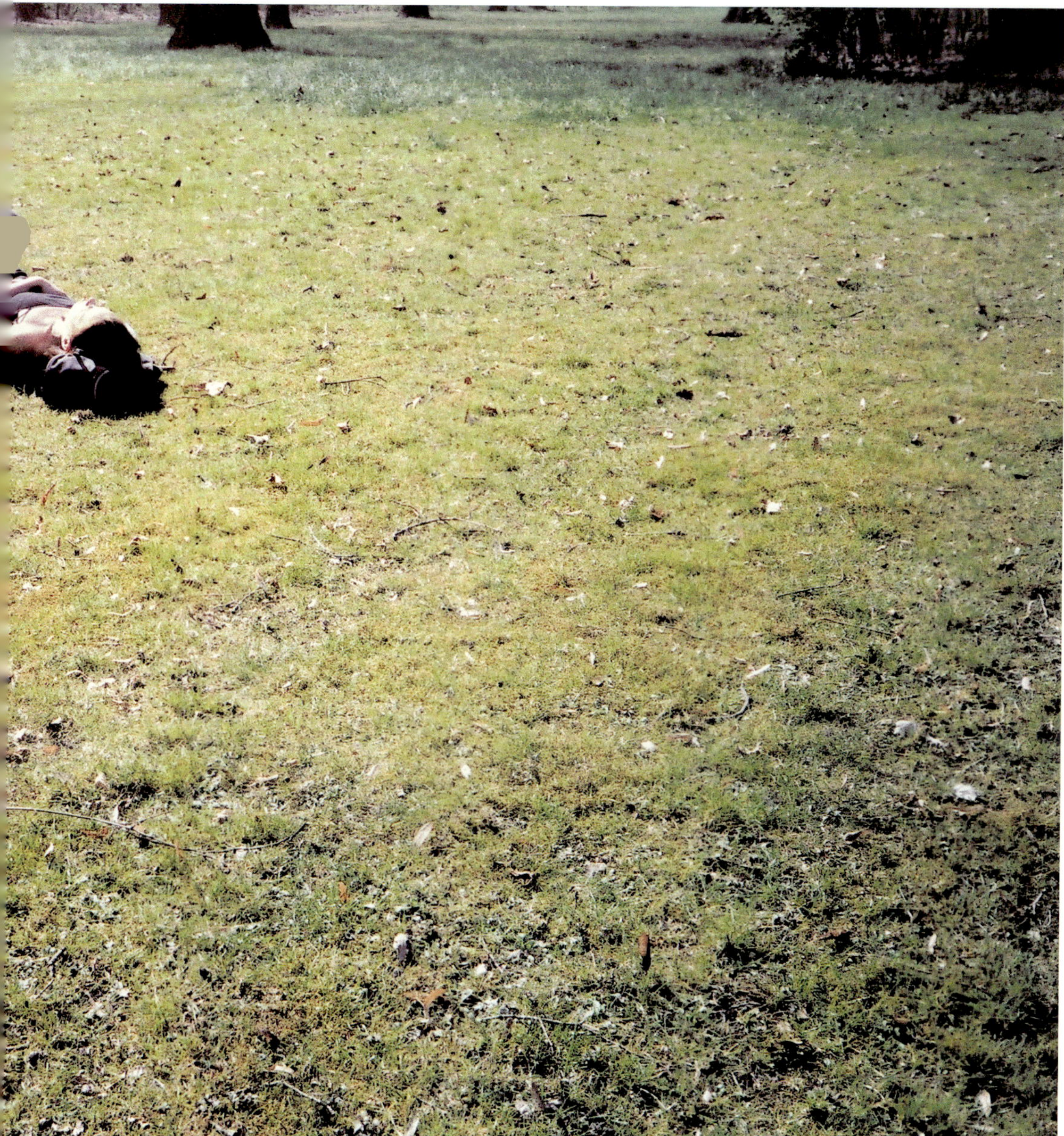

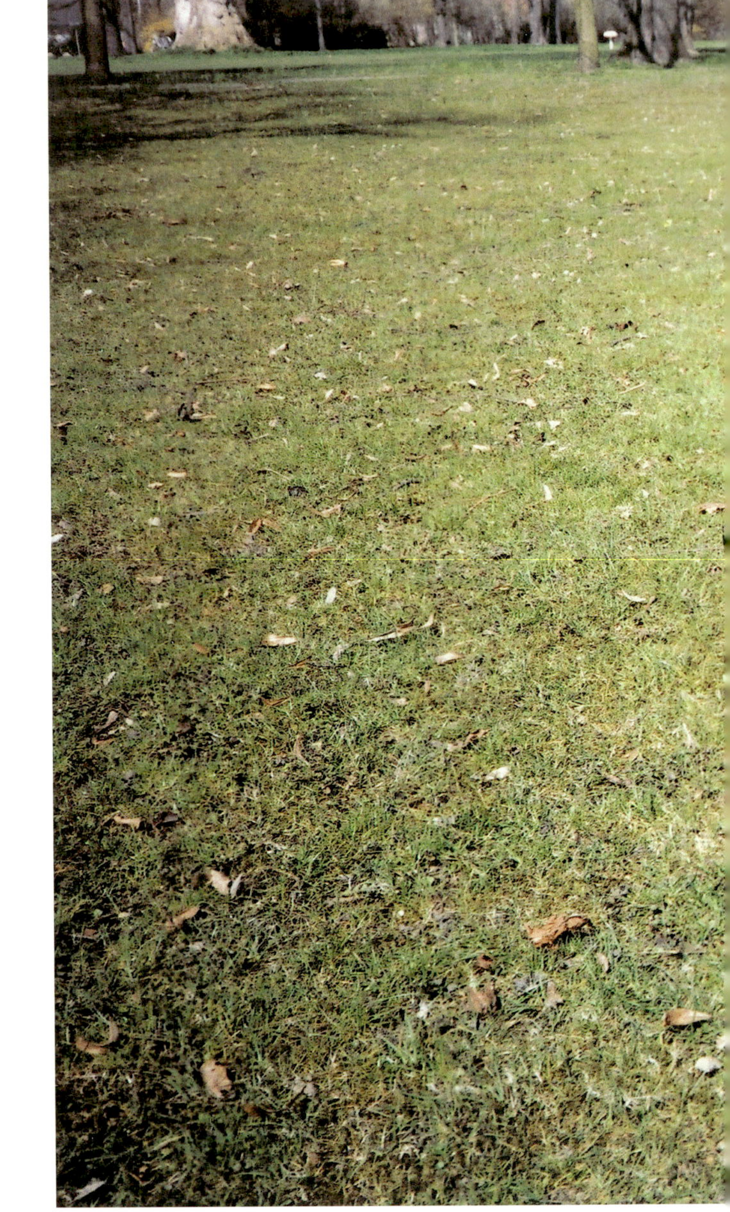

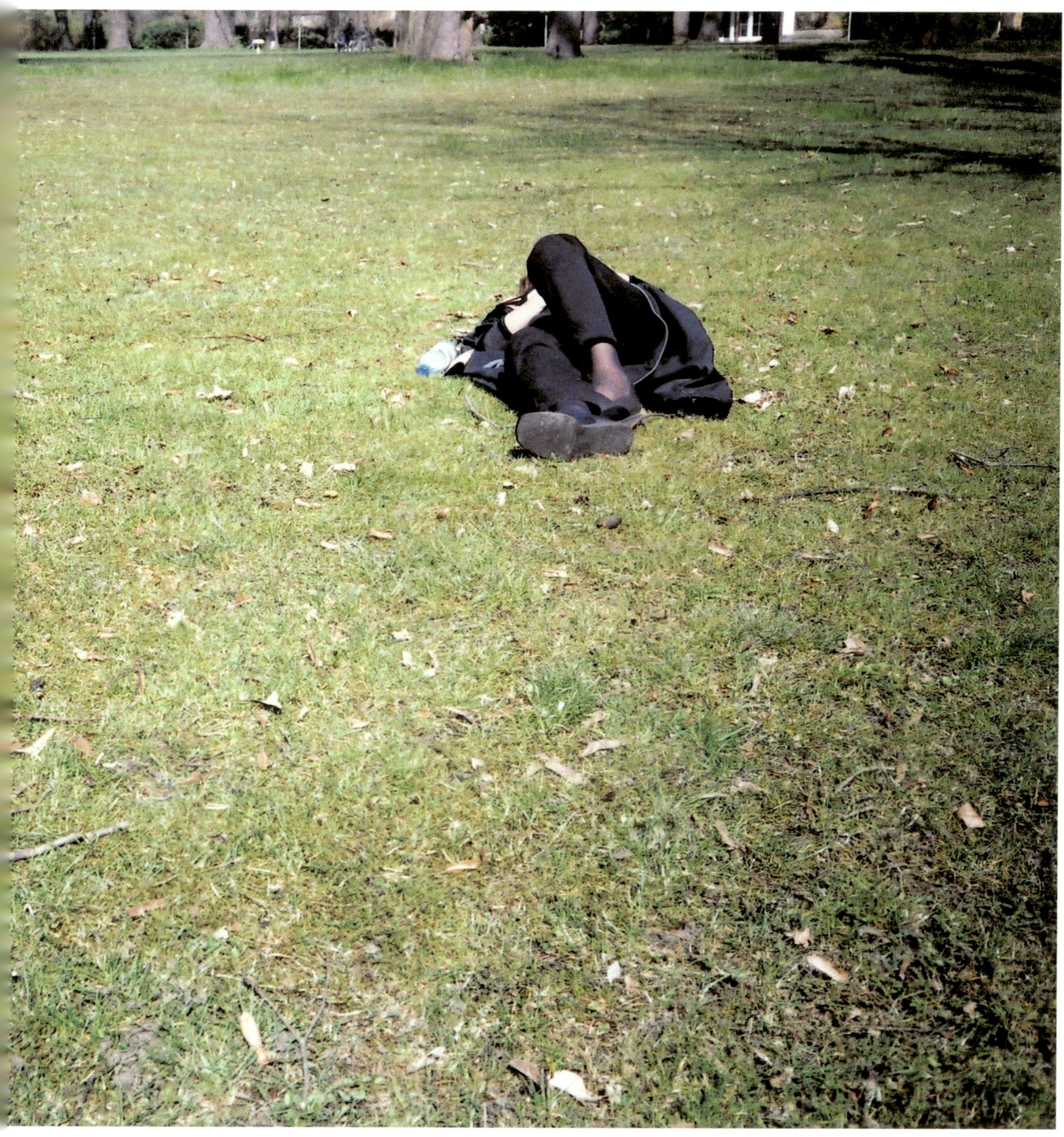

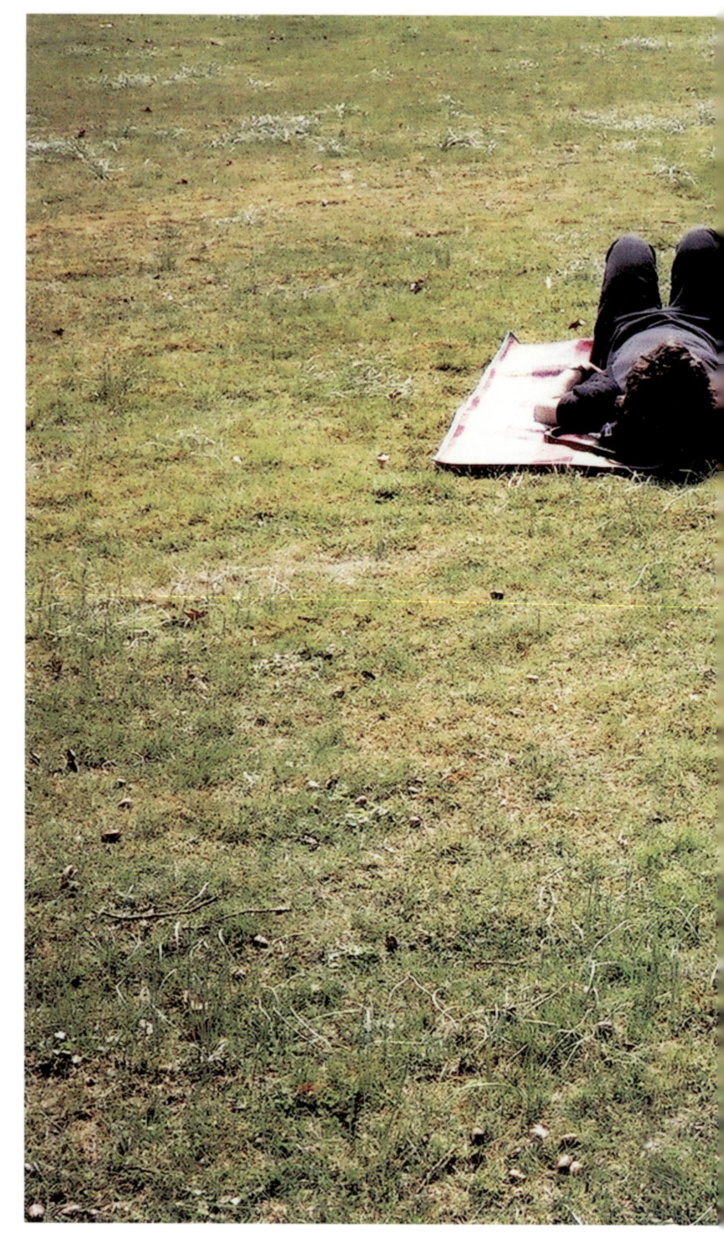

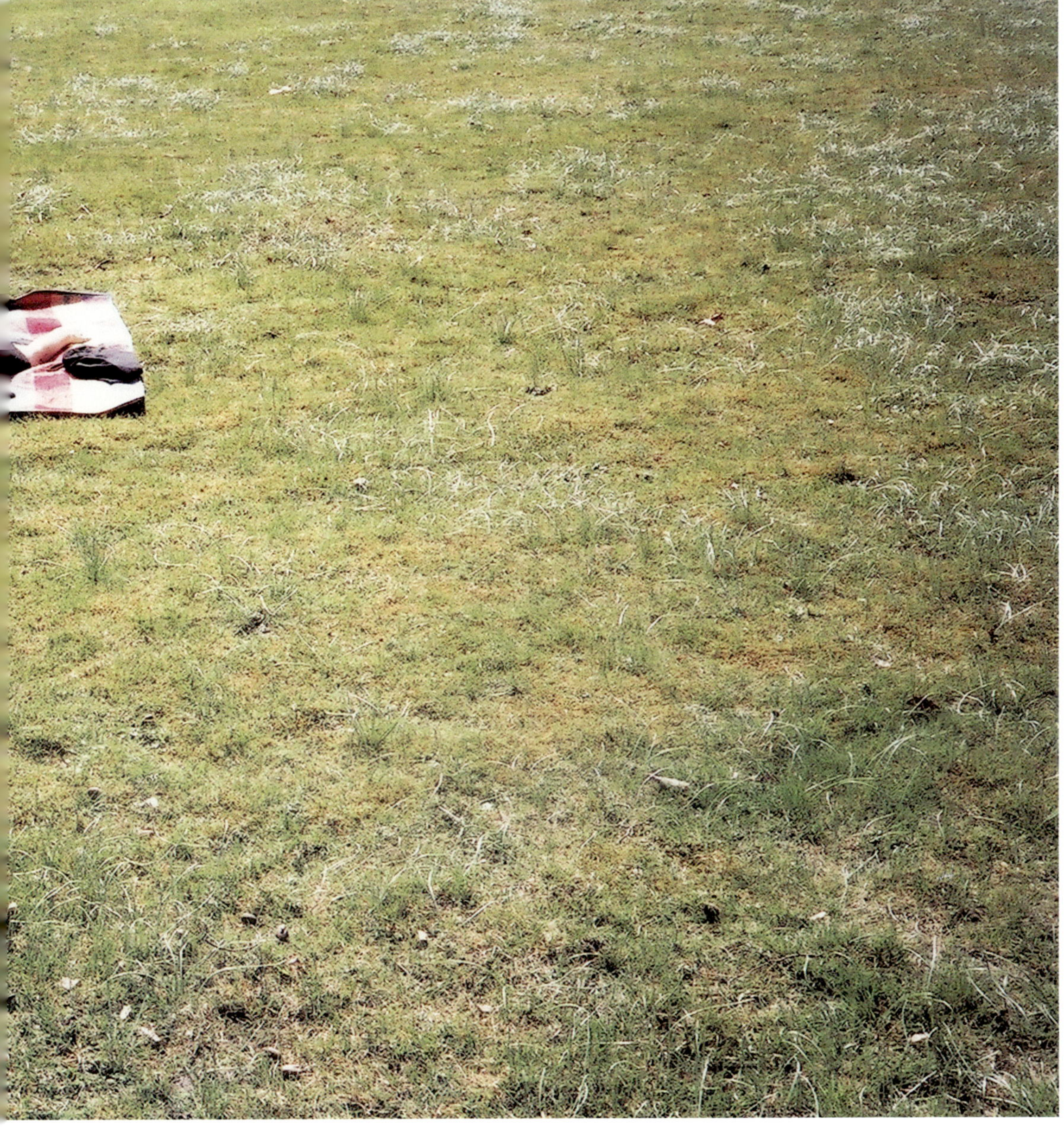

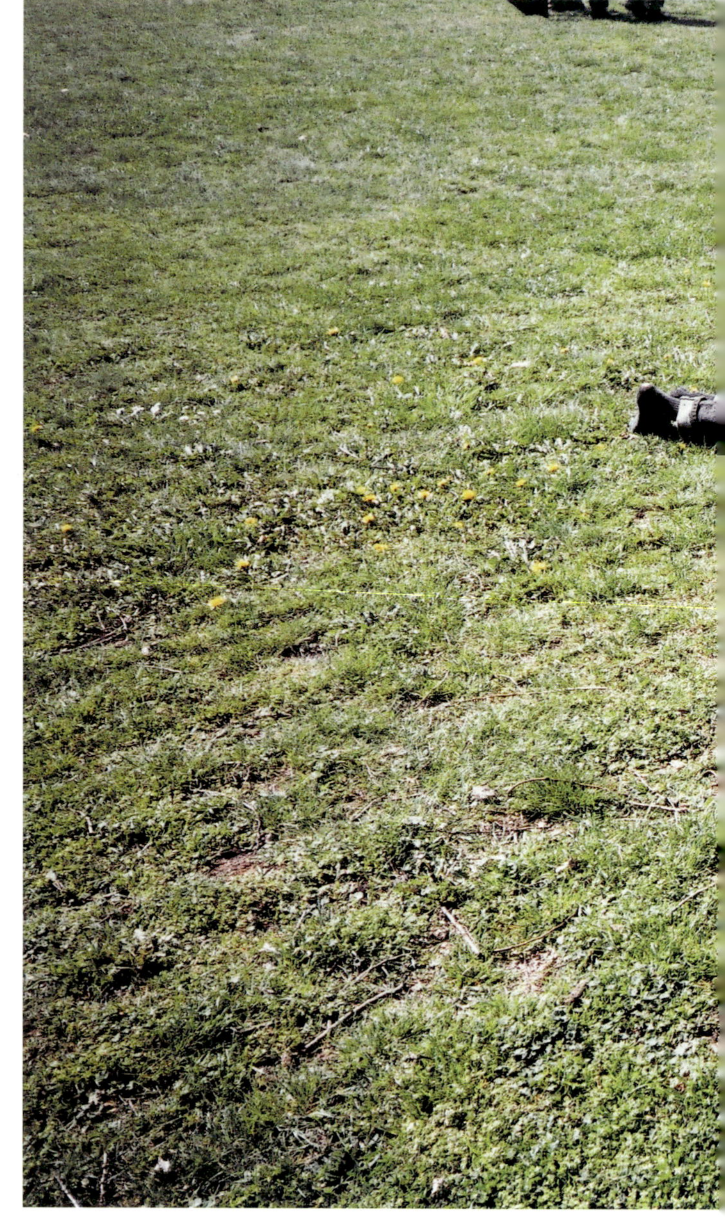

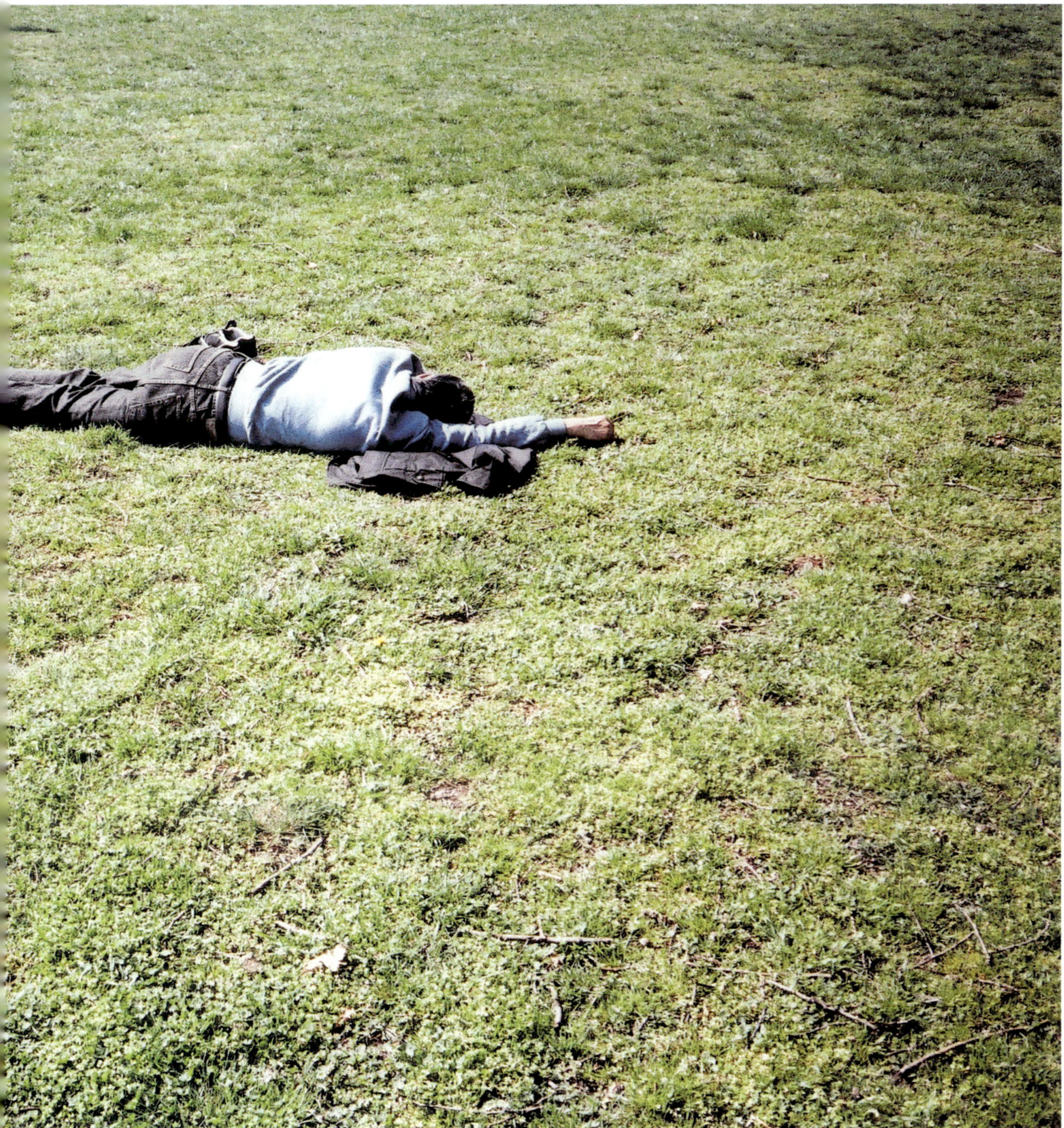

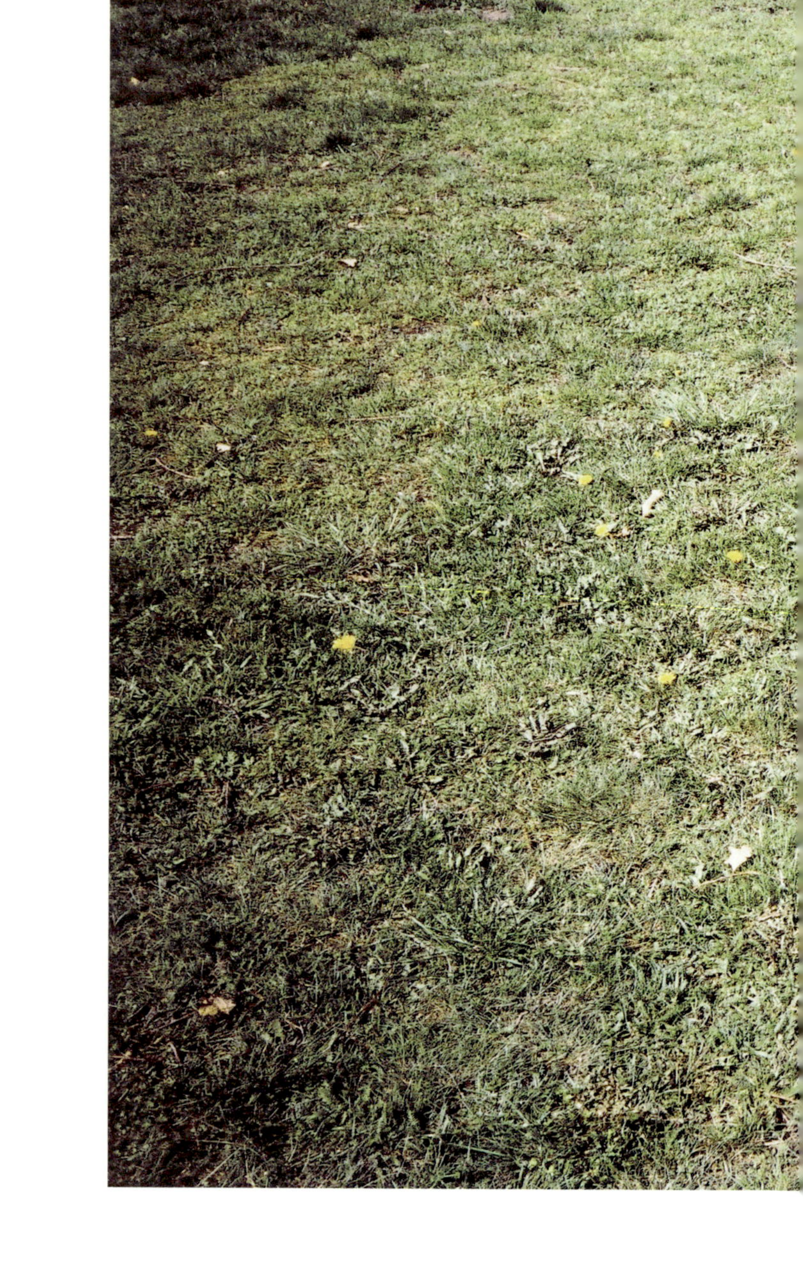

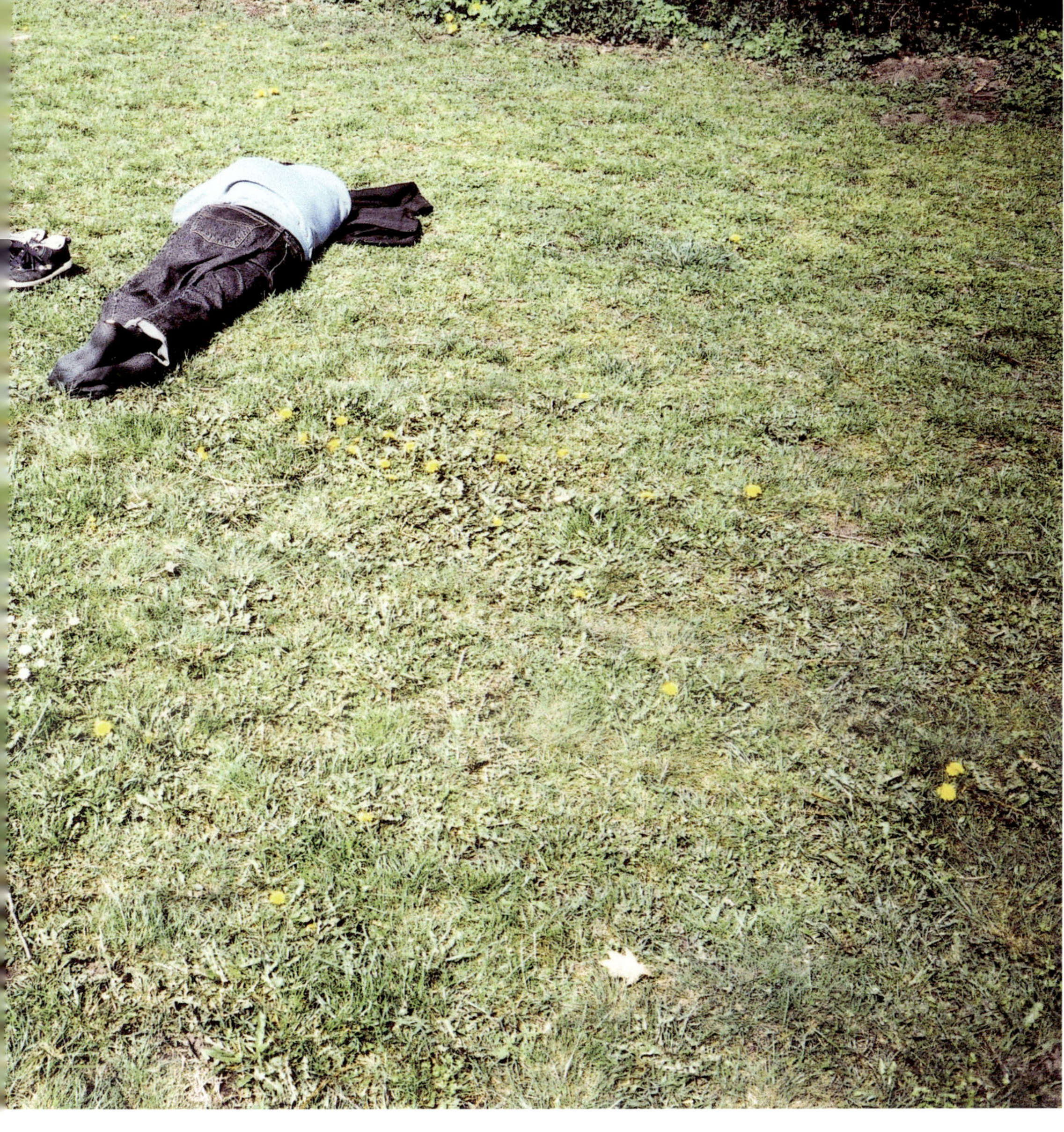

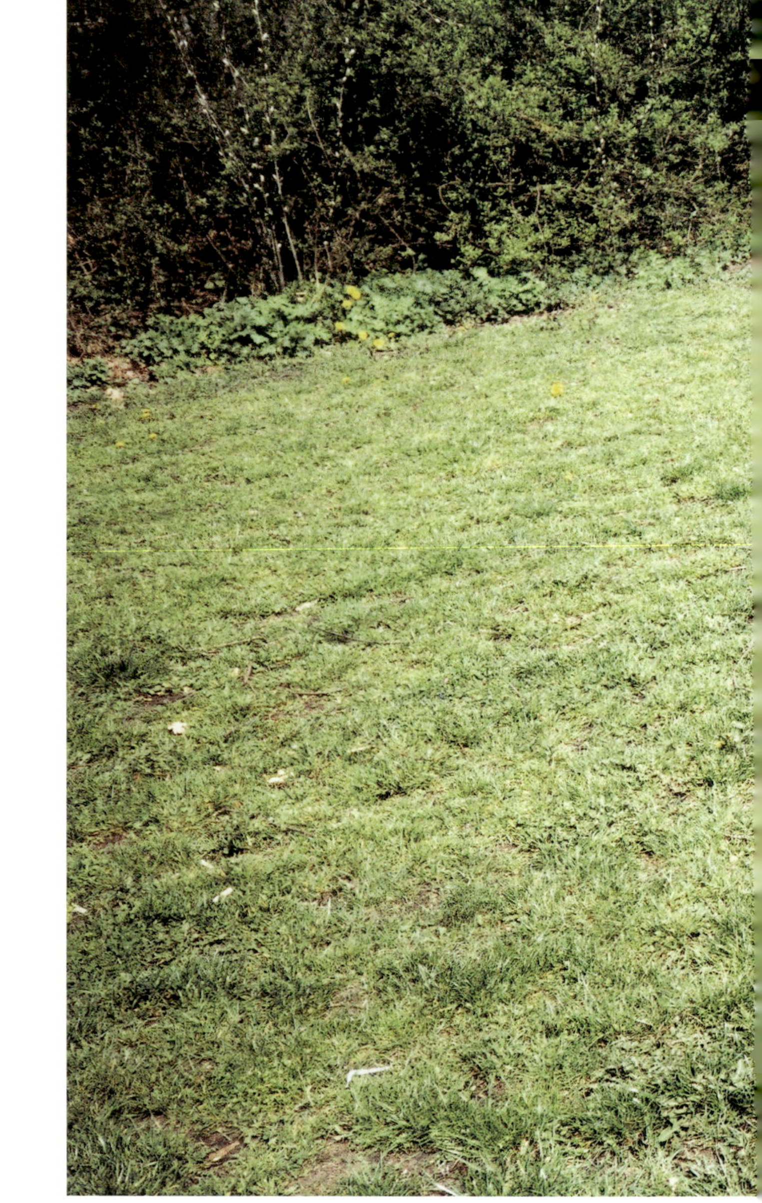

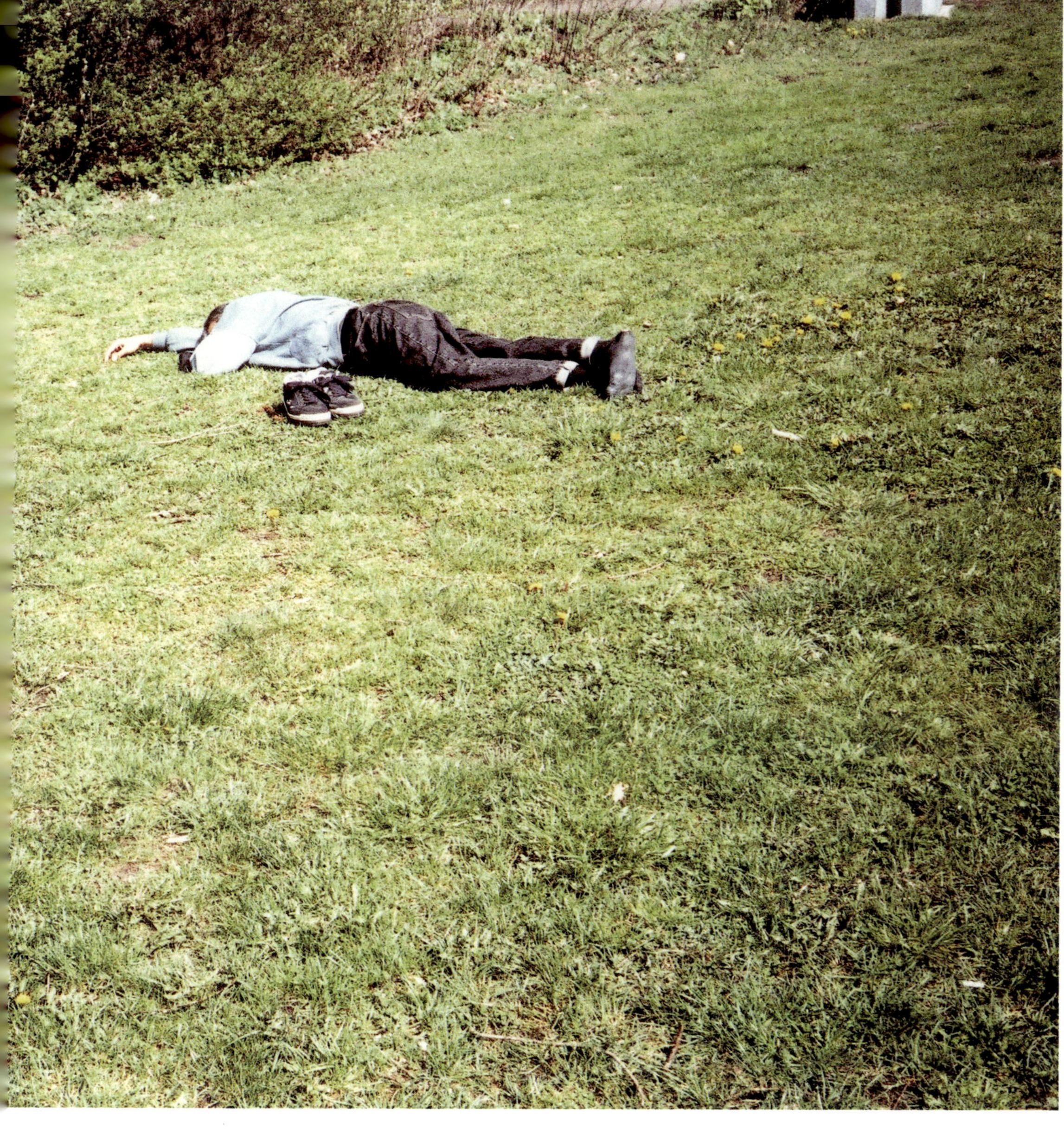

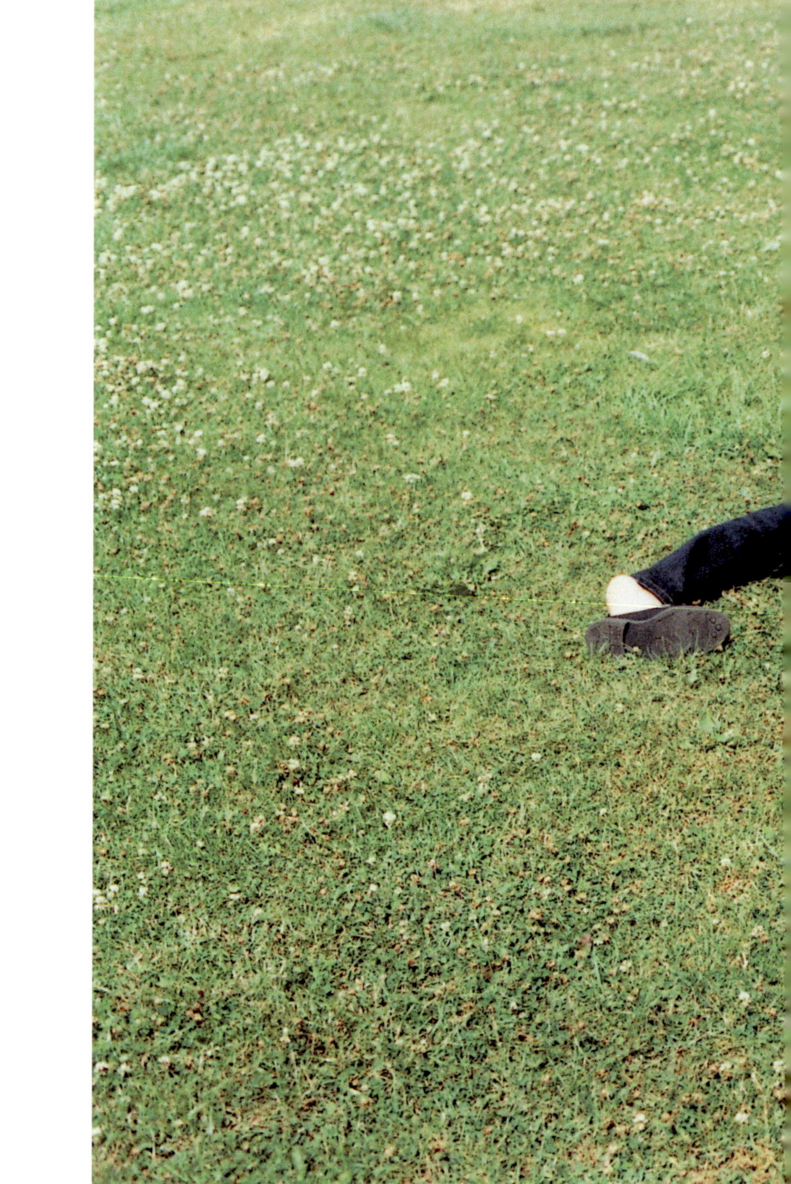

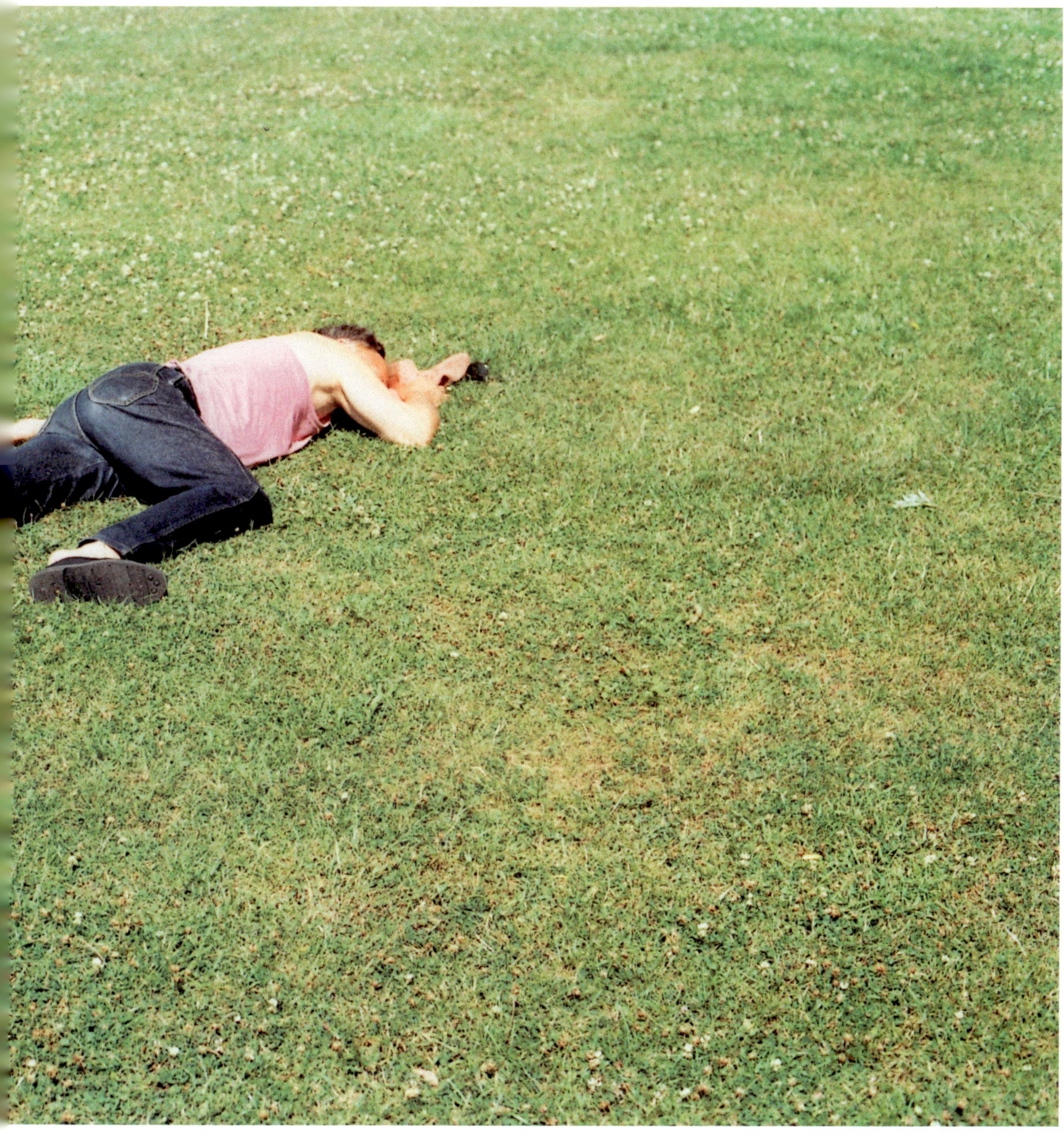

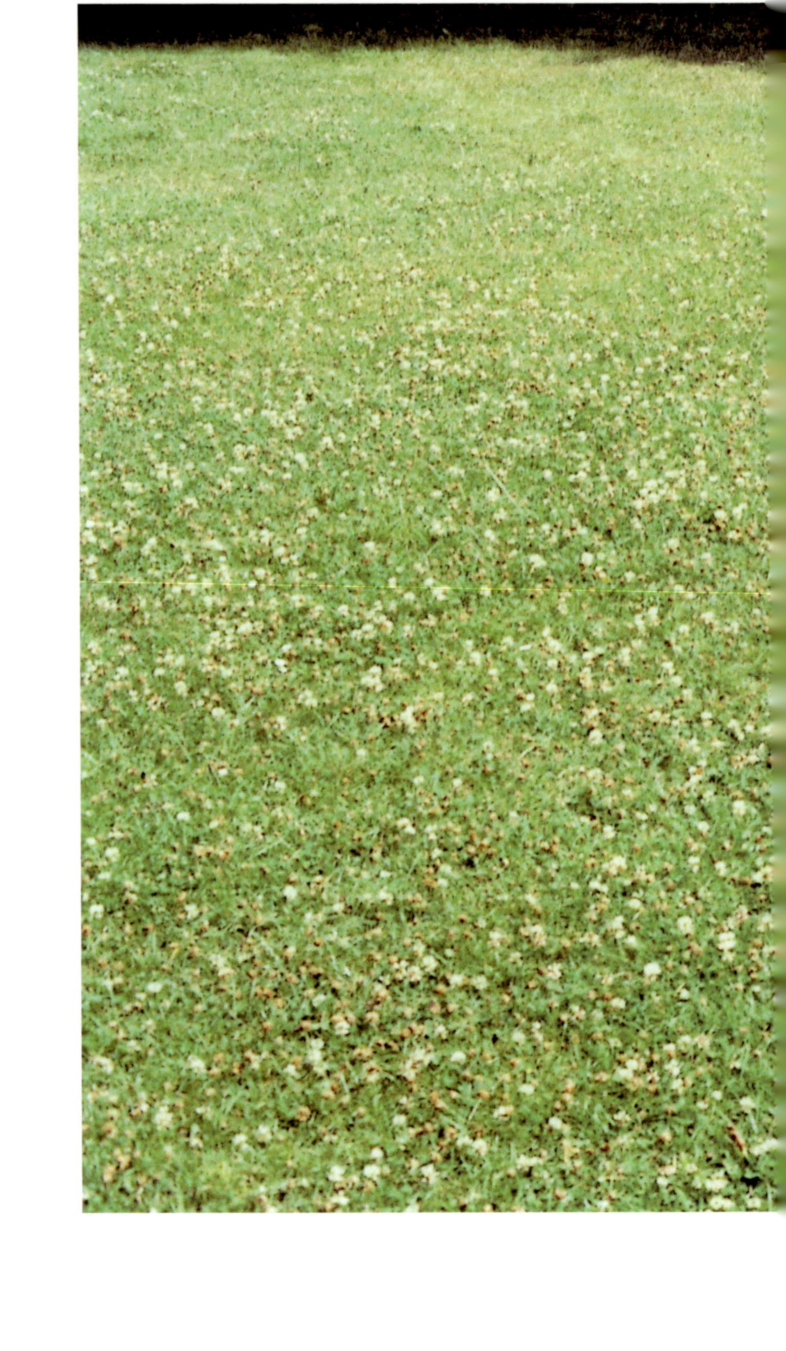

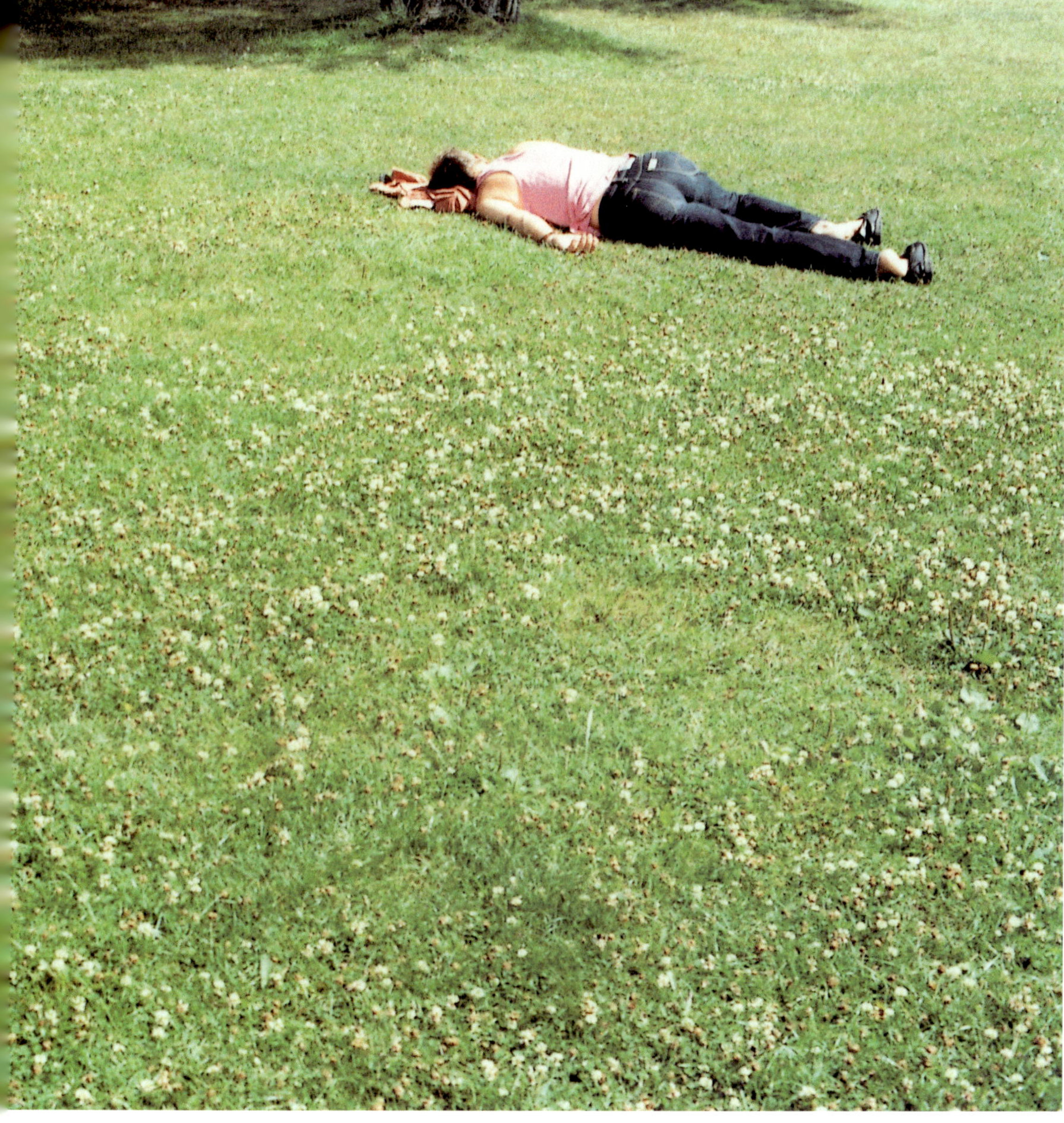

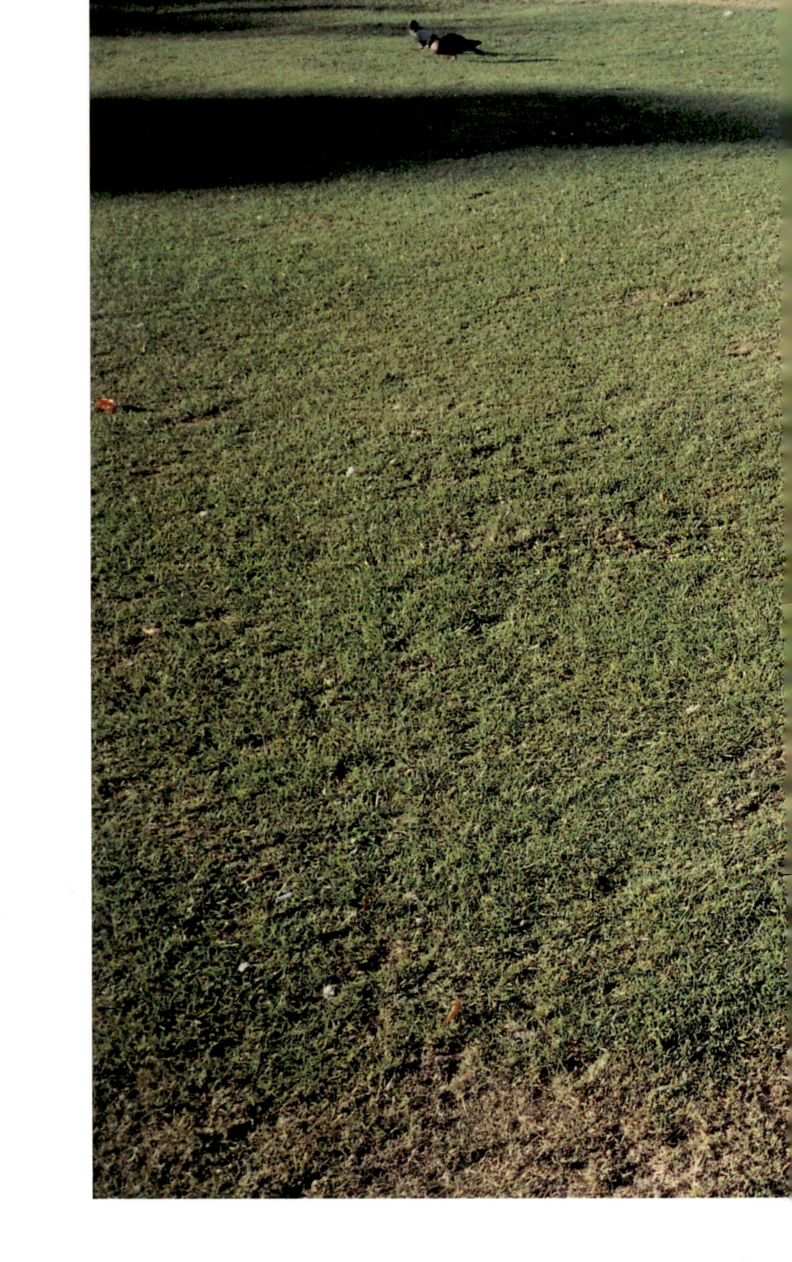

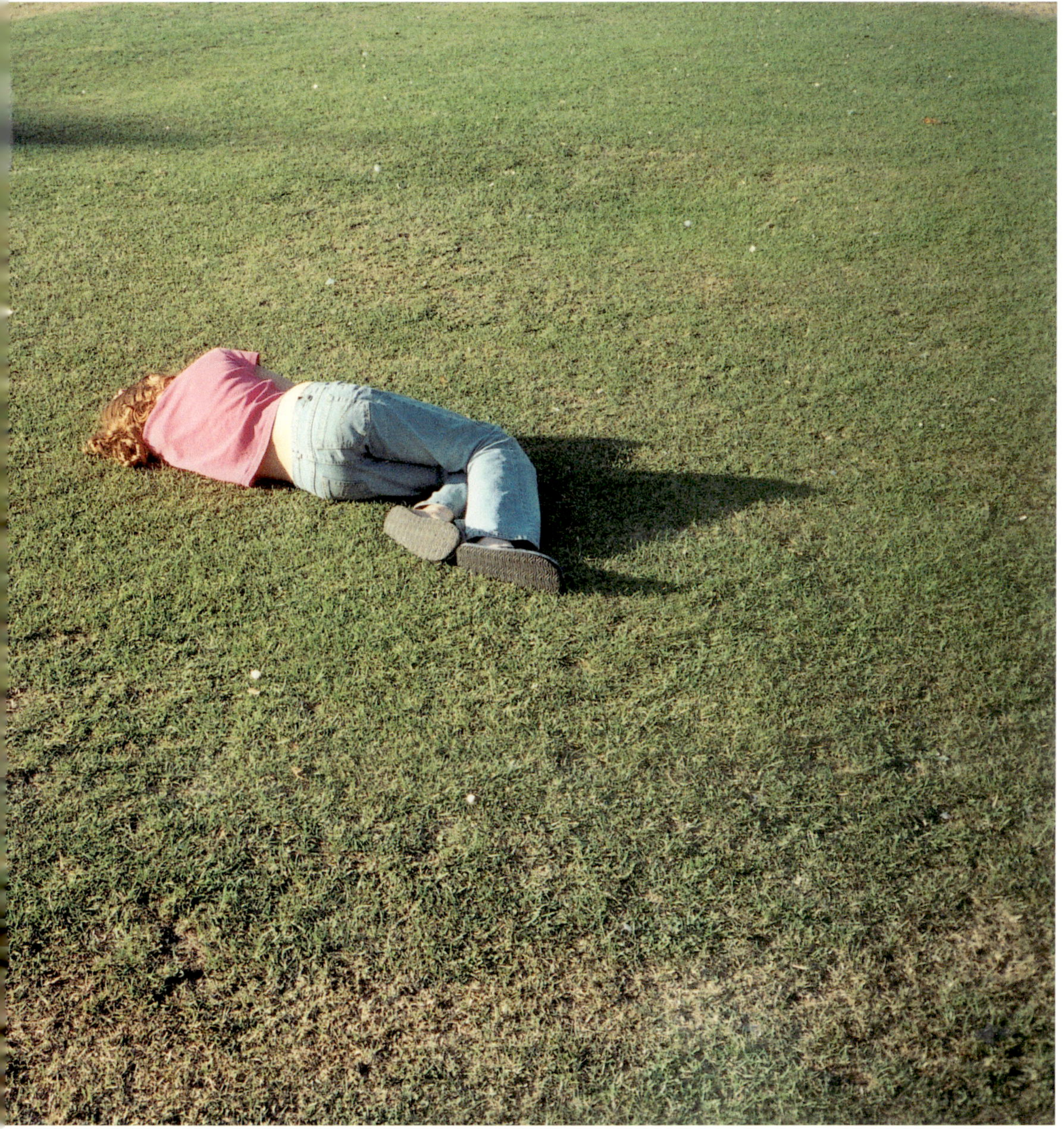

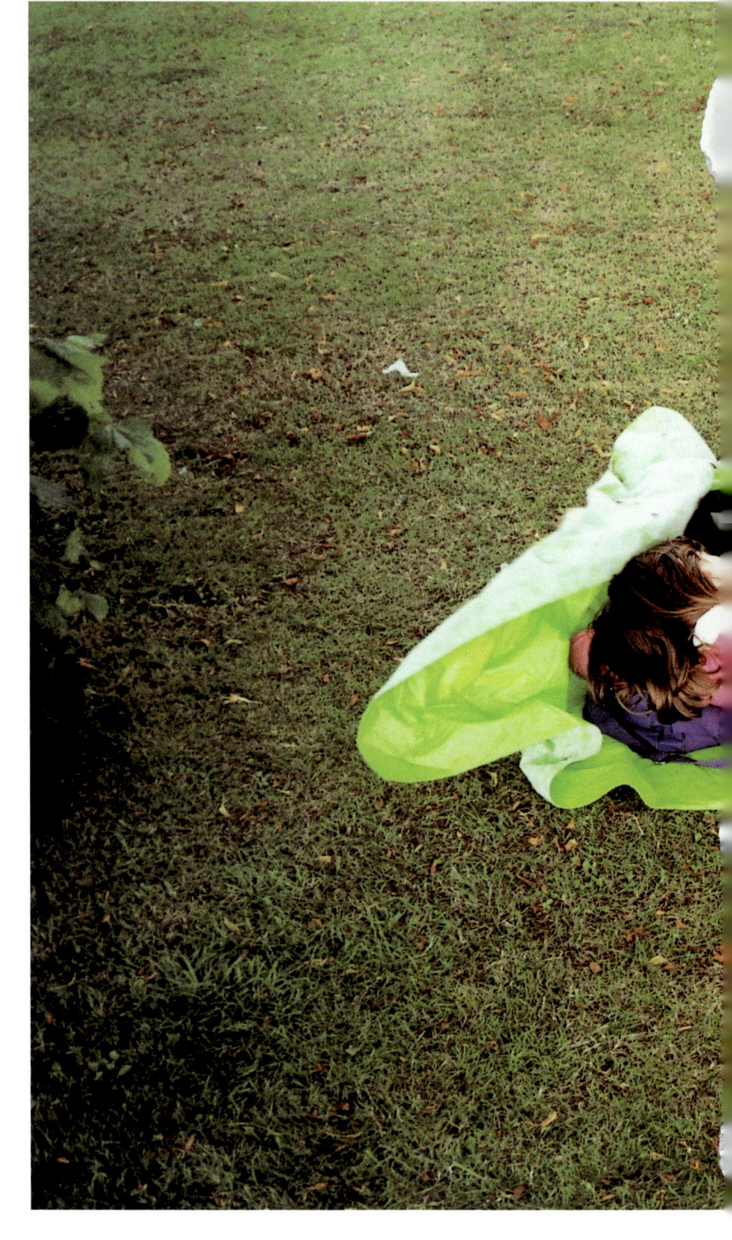

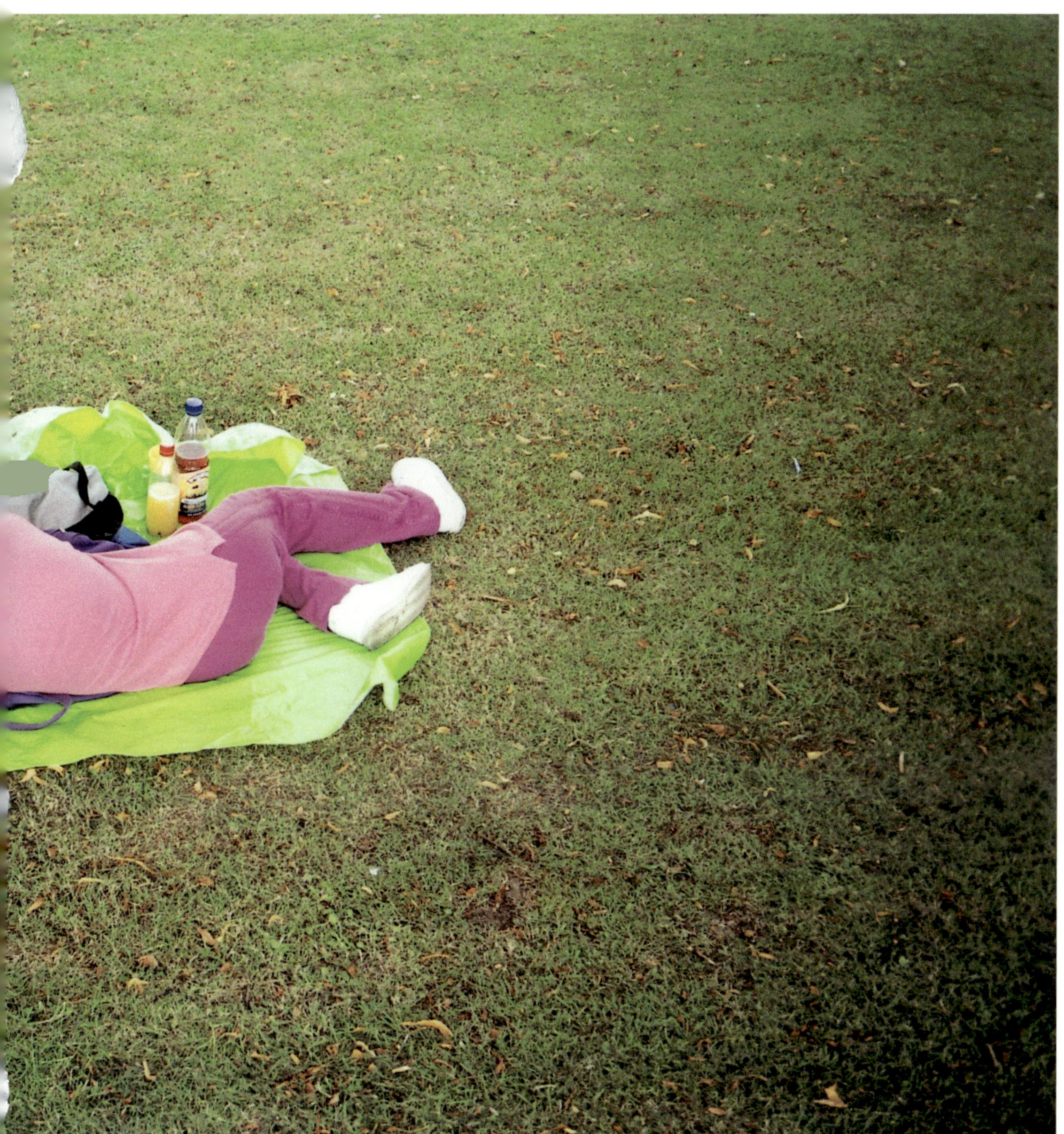

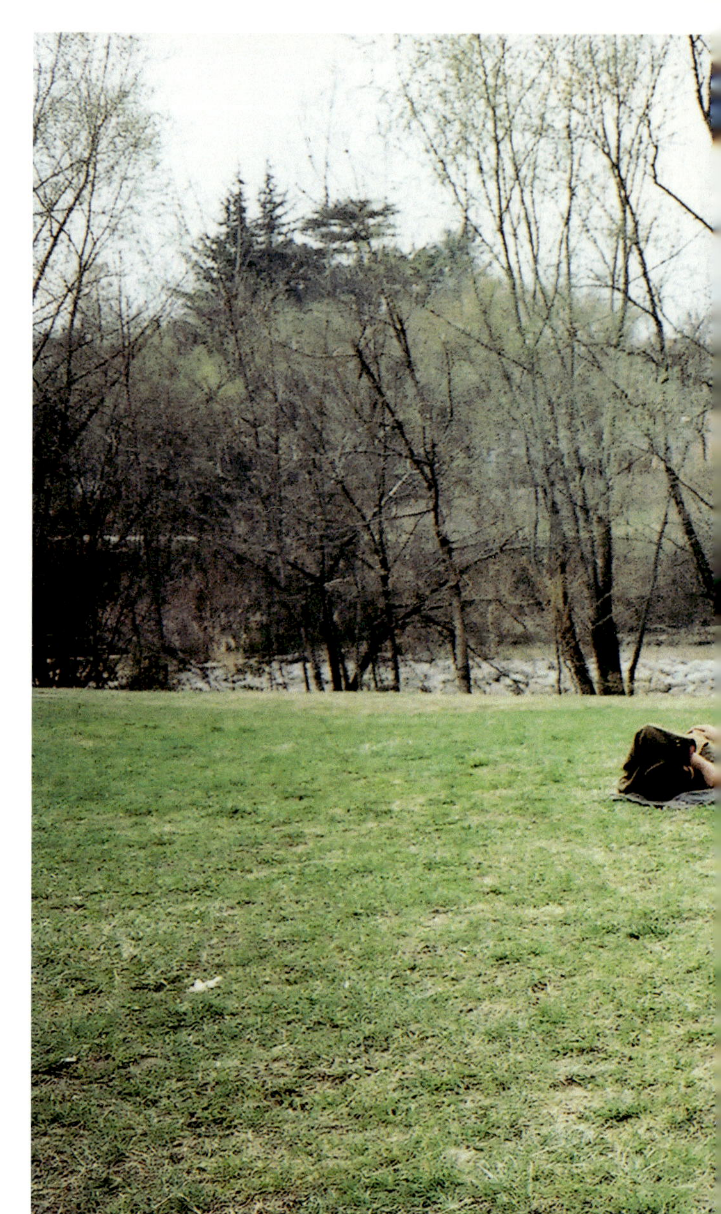

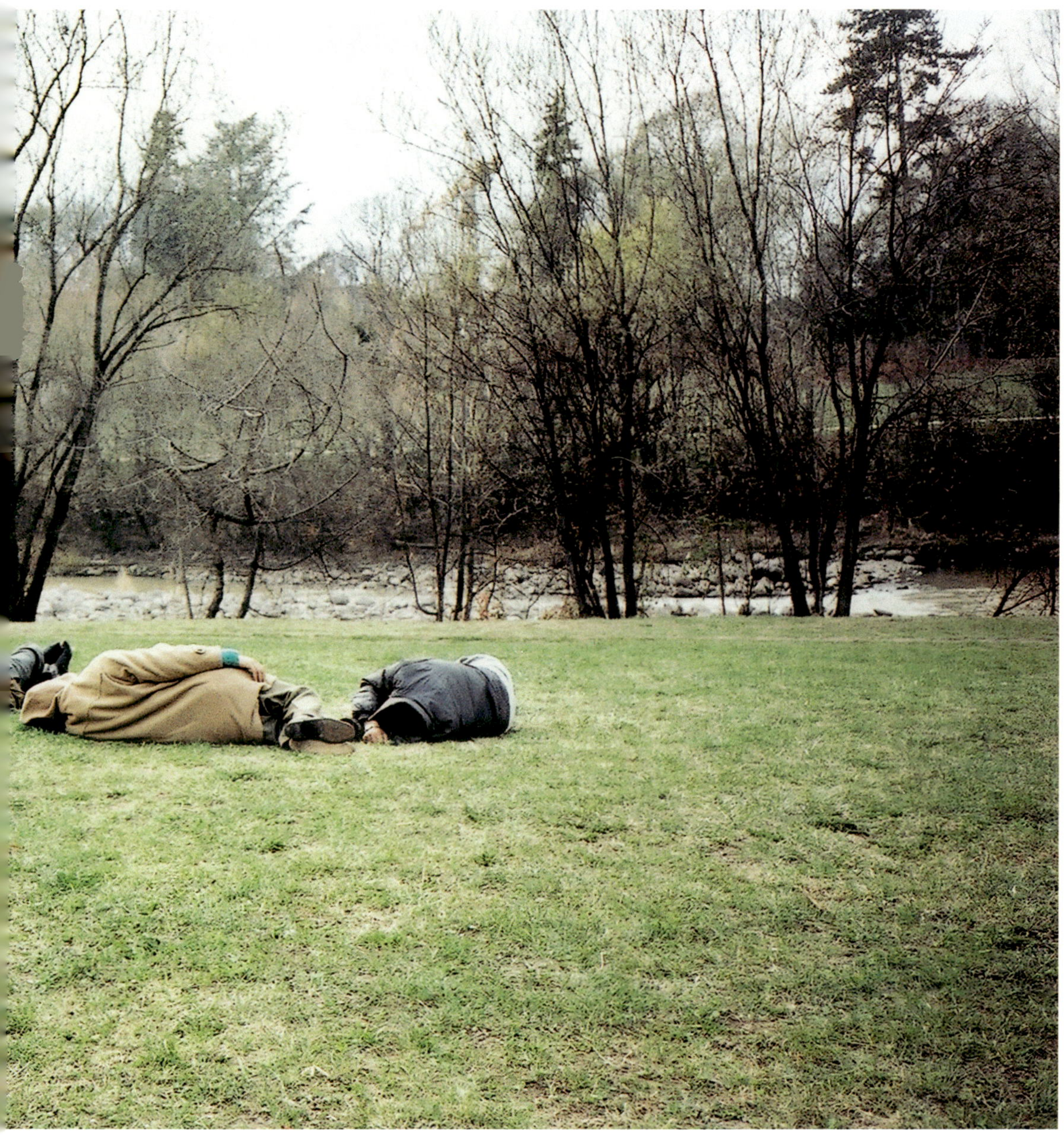

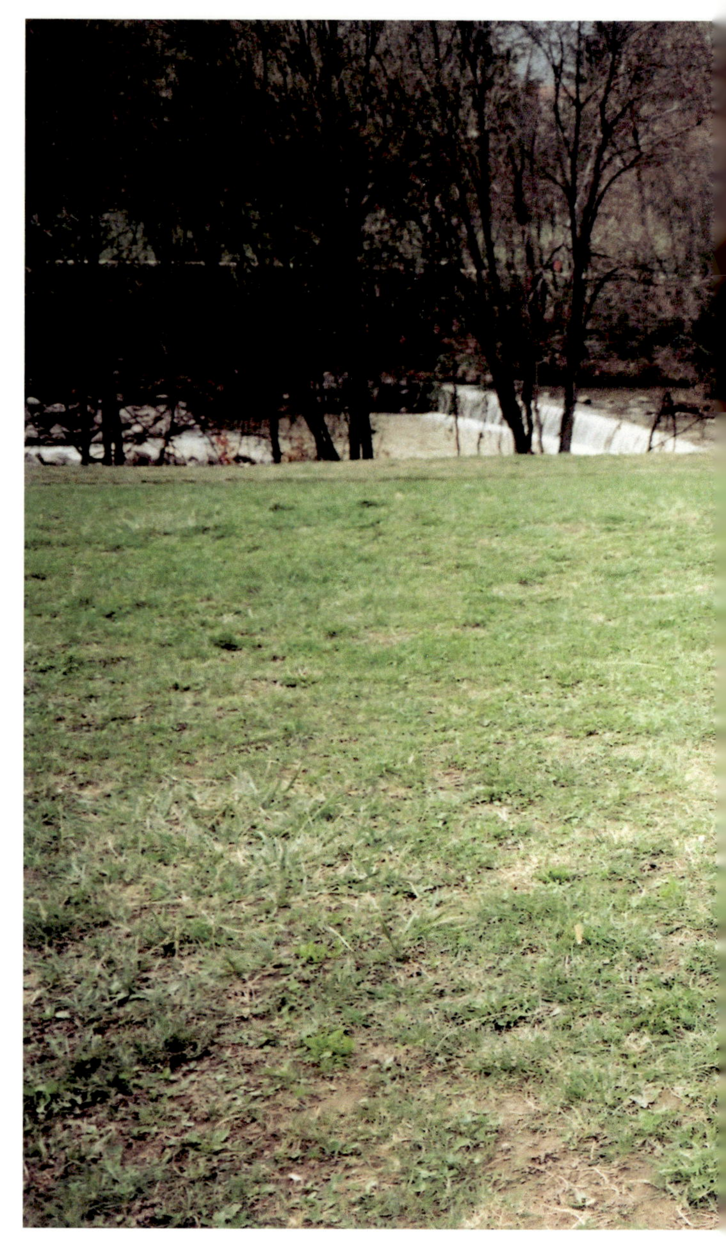

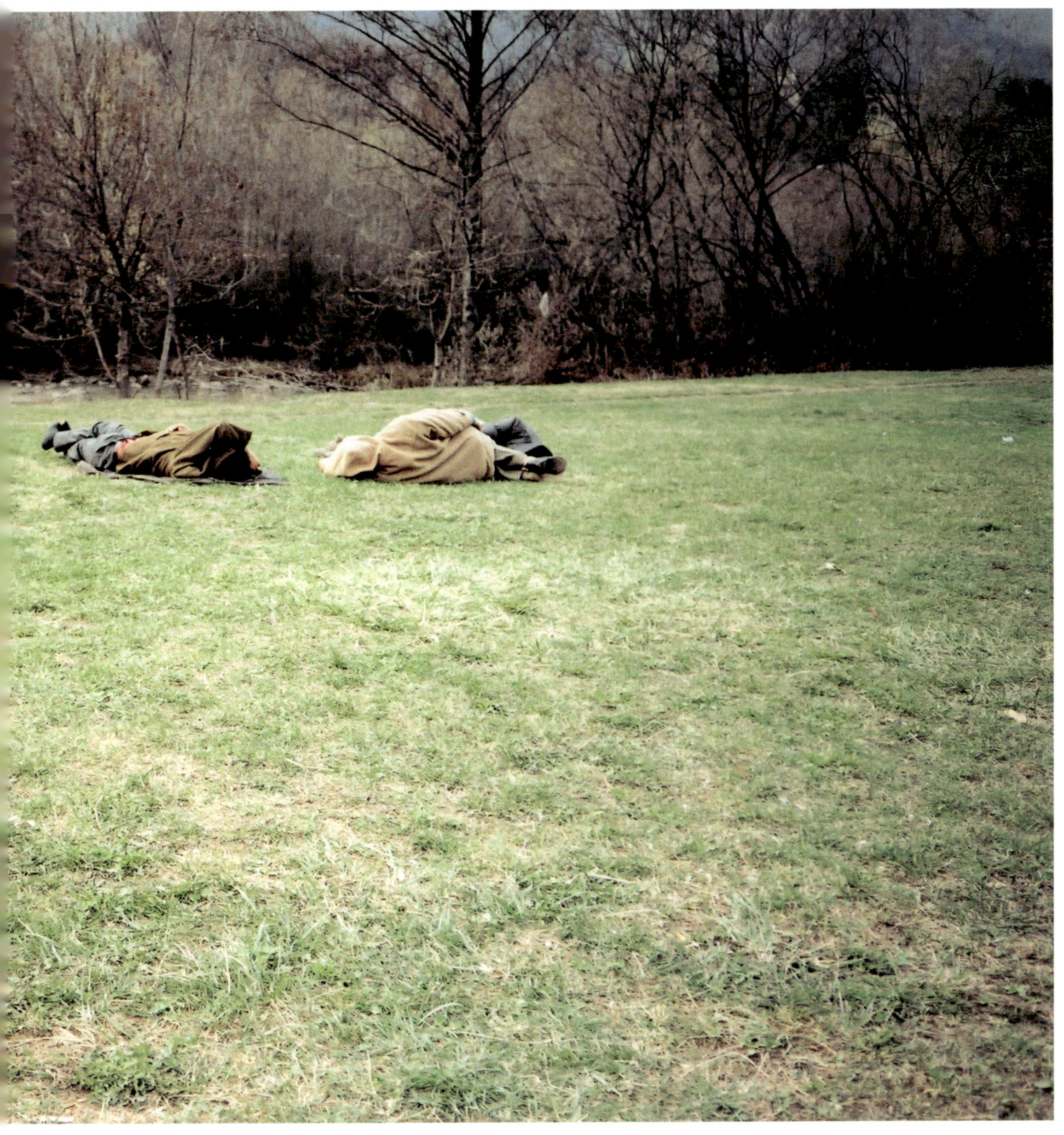

Erik Steinbrecher born March 10, 1963 in Basel, Switzerland.
Attended night courses in art. Completed his studies in architecture.
Lives in Berlin.

Erik Steinbrecher
Gras, Photographs 1993 - 2002

Design: Alex Trüb, Erik Steinbrecher
Printing: Druckerei Odermatt, 6383 Dallenwil

© 2002 for the photographs: Erik Steinbrecher
All photographs: 70.8 x 106.3 cm / 11.8 x 17.7 inches each,
Courtesy Stampa Gallery Basel, info@stampa-galerie.ch
and Barbara Weiss Gallery, Berlin, mail@galeriebarbaraweiss.de

© 2002 for this edition: Edition Patrick Frey
www.editionpatrickfrey.com
c/o Scalo Zürich, Berlin, New York
Head office: Weinbergstr. 22a, CH - 8001 Zürich / Switzerland
www.scalo.com
Distributed by Scalo / Zürich,
D.A.P. / NY and Thames & Hudson / London

Gras was supported by Ricola
and Alfred Richterich Stiftung, Laufen

First edition 2002
ISBN 3 - 905509 - 44 - X
Printed in Switzerland